Mindset of the Successful

7 Powerful and Highly Effective Success Habits Used by Millionaires to Attract Money, Wealth, Growth and Achieve Life Mastery

Written by Tony Ramsey

electronically or in print. This extends to creating a secondary or tertiary copy of the work or a recorded copy and is only allowed with an expressed written consent from the Publisher. All additional rights reserved.

The information in the following pages is broadly considered to be a truthful and accurate account of facts and as such any inattention, use or misuse of the information in question by the reader will render any resulting actions solely under their purview. There are no scenarios in which the publisher or the original author of this work can be in any fashion deemed liable for any hardship or damages that may befall them after undertaking information described herein.

Additionally, the information in the following pages is intended only for informational purposes and should thus be thought of as universal. As befitting its nature, it is presented without assurance regarding its prolonged validity or interim quality. Trademarks that are mentioned are done without written consent and can in no way be considered an endorsement from the trademark holder.

Table of Contents

Introduction

"It takes a different mindset to be successful in anything; that's why there's not a lot of super-duper successful people, because it's guys I know who may be ten times more talented than me, but they don't work as hard." — Rico Love

Before we begin, I'd like you to know that you have two choices before you right now. You either keep doing what you are currently doing to live an average life that doesn't do justice to your potential or bring you the success you truly deserve, or you decide to transform your destiny by living the life of your dreams and accomplishing the glory you truly deserve. Are you ready to unlock your true potential? Tap into your inherent skills, abilities, and gifts to build the ultimate successful life?

This book is packed with proven strategies that have brought people roaring success while bringing small yet solid and actionable changes in their life. However, we can only take the horse up to the well. We can't make it drink the water. Everything begins with your decision to succeed. If you are not happy with your current life or simply want to accomplish more, start by deciding to bring about a transformation in your life.

Remember, you can have the swankiest, most expensive car in the world and the best map but if you don't sit in the driver's seat and drive, buddy you aren't getting anywhere!

If you aren't happy with where you are currently doing or aim for greater success, it's time to reprogram your mind. You'll be amazed at how much you can achieve simply by activating the power of your mindset, thoughts, and beliefs. Bing successful and wealthy begins with a mindset. Often the difference between people who are making a killing and those who are struggling to make ends meet is their mindset. The rich and successful operate with a wealthy mindset.

It doesn't come overnight. It requires small, gradual changes in everyday habits, a shift in thoughts, taking practical steps to move closer to your goals and much more. I'll not just talk in terms of some hyper-exaggerated success guru jargon. My aim is to offer you powerful, practical and actionable tips that work like magic when it comes to channelizing your potential and increasing your chances of success. The pointers mentioned in the book will bring about a paradigm shift in the way you approach your life and work. They will boost your energy, positive thinking and the enthusiasm with which you view your goals.

Let's get this clear. This is not a get-rich or successful-quick handbook. I never recommend that kind of stuff. For me, the crock pot mindset is way more powerful than the microwave mindset. If you want to accomplish long-term wealth, success and mastery, build it gradually, over a period of time. You can get rich using the get rich quick mindset, but I can bet every penny I own that the wealthy won't sustain in the long run. You need a get rich sure strategy that comes from taking one step at a time, consistently. The crockpot mindset takes discipline, effort, perseverance, sweat, time, delaying gratification and much more but I can sure as hell tell you, it lasts! And you want success and money that last.

You have to keep building your structure of success, one brick at a time, one task at a time. One you experience encouraging results, however small they seem, keep going. In the absence of results, we quit! How unfortunate. You were so close to your destination, just a slight detour and you would've reached your destination, but you give up. Lack of results may require a change in mindset, strategy, direction or an altogether different game plan. However, keep going! This is the single most clinching factor between successful and not so successful people. The successful have the vision, courage, and fortitude to chase their dreams with gutso, despite obstacles. Don't allow your own self-limiting beliefs, perceptions, and ideas block your success.

During an experiment in his laboratory, a marine biologist kept a shark in a massive holding tank and then left several small fish into the tank as baits. As expected, the shark was quick to seize and eat the smaller bait fish. Later, the marine biologist placed a clear piece of fiberglass in the tank, leading to two distinct partitions. The shark was placed on one side, while the small bait fish were on the other.

True to its nature, the shark quickly attacked the smaller fish. However, crashed into the glass divider to bounce back! This didn't deter the shark. It kept reaching out to the smaller bait fish only to collide with the fiberglass. After an hour, the shark quit. The biologist repeated this experiment many times over a span of weeks.

Each time, the shark's aggressiveness and the number of attack attempts reduced until the shark stopped going after the small fish out of sheer exhaustion. The biologist eventually removed the divider. However, the shark simply didn't show any will to attack. It was now conditioned to believe that there was a barrier between itself and its food. The fish kept swimming happily free from the shark's attack.

You know what barriers you are dealing with on your way to success? Nope, not your monster boss, frenemy co-workers, government policies, spouse, competitors, etc. etc. Your biggest barrier is your self-limiting mindset! A majority of people, much like the shark, give up after experiencing challenges and setbacks. We condition ourselves to give up and stop trying after a few failures. We let failures define us instead of living our definition of success. We often believe that since we failed in the past, success will continue to elude us even in the future. Couldn't be any further from the truth! We create non-existent barriers in our minds, even when physical barriers don't exist between us and what we want to accomplish in life.

You know the chained elephant syndrome, right? The elephant is a powerful and mighty beast. With one tug of its strength, it can free itself from the chains and ropes that tie its legs to a tree. I mean, we are talking about the largest land mammal. However, it doesn't seem to make any effort to free itself from its chains and just stands there, tied and resigned to its fate. Why? Because since the time the elephant was a baby, it was taught that it couldn't break free from the ropes and chains. Over a period of time, the powerful mammal believed this to be its truth. It could escape simply by showing some strength to shake off the chains. However, the most unfortunate thing is, it didn't know that it could break free from the chains, and therefore surrendered to its fate.

We are pretty much like the elephant. We have it in us to accomplish all the success, wealth and glory we are destined to achieve. However, only a handful live a life of their dreams because the others, like the elephant, don't even know that they are capable of freeing themselves from their current, mediocre lives if they show the strength and fortitude to challenge their self-limiting beliefs.

Almost every success story starts with a mindset. All glorious people believe that they were destined to be rich and successful, which helps them actively work on their goals.

Carol Dweck, a Stanford psychologist, founded the "growth mindset and fixed mindset" concept in her book titled *Mindset: The New Psychology of Success*. One of the best takeaways from the book is that our mindset isn't some far-fetched abstract thought. It is a real concept that can nurture to help you accomplish success, wealth and glory.

Do you possess the elephant's mindset that resigns to its destiny or do you possess a mindset that is constantly looking for opportunities and solutions to release yourself from the chains of a mediocre life to chase the exceptional and extraordinary?

Which of the two mindsets you fall under the will to a certain extent determine your chances of success and destiny. Debbie Millman aptly said,

"If you imagine less, less will be what you undoubtedly deserve."

Plenty of research has been dedicated to the influence of thoughts and beliefs in our conscious as well as a subconscious mind on our actions, and eventually destiny. We aren't as limited by our external circumstances as we are by a fixed mindset, which prevents us from moving outside our comfort zone.

The typical traits of a fixed mindset person are – they tend to believe everything from their intelligence to creativity to abilities is static. In their mind, it is impossible to transform, enhance and sharpen it meaningfully to accomplish greater success. They operate with constricted beliefs that things can never get greater than they are. Everything is pre-determined, and there is a huge fear of failure, which paralyzes them into inaction. This is their way of maintaining their current position, which prevents them from climbing greater heights of success. A typical fixed mindset stand is, "Oh! I'll appear completely foolish if I try something new and fail." This is a glaring fixed mindset philosophy.

The growth mindset doesn't hold a desire to be accepted or validated. It is more driven by a desire for passion, results, moving beyond one's comfort zone and taking calculated risks. Constantly pushing the envelope and raising the bar is the hallmark of a growth mindset. People with a fixed mindset don't believe in sticking to safe, cushy paths. Rather, they take on unexplored terrains that help them tap into their fullest potential and accomplish greater success.

Unfortunately, a majority of people don't even know that they are capable of accomplishing great success and wealth if they display the strength to act in the right direction. Don't be the elephant that is resigned to a less than glorious destiny. Gather the strength to move beyond past failures, self-limiting beliefs, and other people's perception to achieve the greatness you are destined for and deserve.

Here are seven powerful, proven and action-worthy habits that have the potential to transform your life forever!

Your wealth, success, and life mastery await you!

Chapter One: Success Habit One - Define Your "Why"

"He who has a why can endure any how." – Frederick Nietzsche

Yes, you want to accomplish certain dreams and goals, which is why you are reading or hearing this book. However, do you know why you want it? For instance, I asked one of one of my clients why they wanted to launch a business. He stated in a very matter of fact manner that they wanted a big house, a swish car and the best vacations money could buy. I repeated my question. Again, he said because he wanted all the material possessions he mentioned above. I asked him for the third time, and he lost all patience by now and snapped at me. I calmly told him, he was only mentioning materials possessions or the means to an end, which were not really his end. Then, something struck him, and he quickly realized his folly and said, "Because I want to give my family the best life possible."

What is your "why" that will drive you towards your goals with the right zeal, motivation, and enthusiasm? When you define your "why" the "how" invariably chalks its path. You have to know why you want to accomplish something or what is the higher purpose or reason for accomplishing something before you can chase it with all you have. Your why keeps you on course in choppy waters, it will help you stay strong and motivated when the going gets tough. Each of us has a "why" that needs to be discovered, and not everyone has the same "whys." Someone may work hard for the bigger purpose of giving their children a good life and education; others may work hard to travel around the world. Still, others may work hard because it is their dream to open an art school. Each of us has a distinct why that drives us. Identifying your why is the first and most important step to achieving success, wealth and life mastery.

Defining your why at the outset is important because each time you are tempted to throw in the towel in the face of obstacles, your "why" will prevent you from doing it. When challenges knock you down, it will allow you to get up, shake the dust and continue your efforts. Your "why" will sustain you in the long run!

The "why" gives you a value-centric and purposeful life. Define your "why" clearly. Why do you want to do something – financial freedom, more time with family, travel around the world, give a good life to your loved ones, start an NGO, open a dance school or are simply passionate about your goal! The why is integral to your success! Even when figuring out the how the "why" plays a huge role. How badly do you want something is determined by your "why" and if your "why" is strong, you are unstoppable. Being a hustler and 'goal digger' comes easy when your "why" is in place.

We've all played video games, right? They are a fantastic analogy for life itself. There are multiple levels, obstacles and energy boosters/life givers! Hell, if I put aside a penny for the number of times I've got thrown off the course by the obstacles, I'd own a gold charter plane by now. We face monsters and enemies trying to throw us off guard. However, we don't give up playing. Your resolve to win deepens with every defeat, and you play until you knock down those enemies and obstacles. Life isn't any different really!

If you have a powerful "why," you continue playing instead of quitting. If you have a powerful "why," you will not just try to pass classes but to ace them! With strong "why," you won't simply work to pay your bills but will make enough to travel around the world. You "why" will not just help you write a screenplay that gets made into a movie, you'll write an Oscar-winning screenplay. The difference between success/excellence and failure/mediocrity is often a "why." If you haven't already defined your "whys," do it now!

You can't calm every storm that comes in your way. However, you can calm yourself to preside over the storm, and the storm will eventually pass.

Knowing your why awards you the filter to wield choices and decisions about your personal and professional life to gain greater fulfillment in everything you do.

Irrespective of whether you are a businessman, an employee, a team leader, a freelancer, an intern, student or whoever - you want a clear why to inject passion into your work. Without purpose or passion, you are likelier to give up when the course gets rough. Those who operate with a solid "why" possess the ability to not just do great work but also inspire those around them. This is because people with a powerful "why" are very driven.

I'll let you in on one of the most unfortunate aspects of human existence. A majority of people live their life by accident. Things will happen to them by chance. We take things as they come, going with the flow, living as this happen on autopilot mode. This is merely surviving or existing, not living. Living comes with fulfillment, which in turn is a result of purpose. When you derive a sense of fulfilment from your purpose, you keep going. You don't simply exist, you live. You don't act to survive, you act go conquer.

Today's work life isn't a cakewalk. You get up early. Drive to work. Deal with a pesky boss and at times even peskier co-workers. Then you hustle to make money, spend sleepless nights trying to complete a deadline. Rinse. Repeat. There are plenty of challenges to deal with on a day to day basis. The

The work world can be tough: Wake up, go to work, deal with the boss, make money, come home, manage your personal life, go to bed, wake up, repeat. That's plenty to deal with every day. Why get fancy by trying to also understand why you do what you do? Your "why" will prevent you from functioning on autopilot mode where things happen to you. Instead, with a clear purpose, you will make things happen.

When you identify your "why," you are able to seek greater clarity, discipline, and confidence to make choices about your relationships, career, communities and other institutions. You will aim to inspire and be inspired in everything you do.

Do you want to wake up each morning with infectious energy, enthusiasm, and passion for work? Do you want to get home feeling fulfilled at the end of every single day? The secret is - WHY.

If you've faced a considerable crisis in life, you would've experienced the power of having a purpose. You'll tap into inexhaustible reserves of energy, courage, perseverance, and determination that you were not even aware you possessed.

When your mission is clear, you'll have laser-like focus. Think of the purpose as the light energy focused via a magnifying glass. When the light is diffused, it is useless. However, when the same light energy is concentrated via a magnifying glass, it can set the paper on fire. Focus it even more with a laser beam and the light energy can slice steel.

Similarly, a clear purpose lets you concentrate all your efforts on priorities, on things that matter the most. It will push you to take risks and move ahead, regardless of obstacles and setbacks.

What is the major difference between humans and animals? Humans, unlike animals, desire much more from their life than just survival. Without answering the question what are we surviving for? You'll be overcome by feelings of depression, despair, and disillusionment if you don't have a purpose!

Ever wondered why there is an alarming increase in the instances of substance abuse, suicide and mental ailments like depression? Or a growing dependence on anti-depressants? The likeliest reason is lack of purpose and true meaning.

You know you are doing something, but you don't know why you are doing it. People are wealthier today than they've ever been yet unfortunately here's a huge gap between well placed and well-being. This is because wealth alone is pointless without a lack of purpose.

A new hire once went to the HR manager and stated that we weren't keen to continue working in the organization. When questioned by the HR personnel, he stated that the workplace was filled with negativity where people talk badly about each other, engage in politics and gossip.

The HR guy then told him that he could leave the organization if he fulfilled one task sincerely. He was to take a glass full of water and walk around the office thrice without spilling a single drop. After completing the task, the employee could leave, the HR stated.

The new recruit got to work immediately and walked thrice around the office without spilling a single drop on the floor. He went to the HR and told him he had successfully completed the task. The HR then questioned him about whether he heard other employees talk badly about each other, gossip or create disturbances. He replied in the negative. The HR also asked him if anyone looked at him in a negative manner. The recruit again replied in the negative.

The HR then went on to tell the new recruit that he had a clear goal to avoid spilling water, which was directly linked to his purpose of wanting to quit the organization. The same is true with our life. When we have a clear purpose, we focus on our priorities instead of other people's negatives or mistakes!

All the people I know realize that they've got to work really hard, and many of them work hard! However, only a handful of them knows what they truly want to accomplish from the hard work. How do plan to get anything in life if you don't even know what you want or what you are working for? Will you reach your destination if you don't enter an address in your GPS? Money isn't really a well-defined goal. How will you realize you've made sufficient money to fulfill your goal of making more money? How much is more? Does more money translate into a private jet, an expensive car or vacations aboard every six months? Setting clear goals or whys awards you the gratification of knowing that your goals are fulfilled when you accomplish them. Let your whys be crystal clear and well-defined.

There is no pathway or thumb rule for identifying your "why." There are several ways through which you can gain greater insights about your life's purpose by knowing yourself and developing a larger understanding of how you can contribute to the world. What can you offer? What is your main value proposition? These and several other questions will help you discover your purpose. To help you find the sweet spot of your "why," here are some questions to ask yourself.

1. What are your inherent strengths?

In the book The Element, author Sir Ken Robinson aptly states that our true element is the sweet point at which our innate talent and skill merge with personal passion. When a person is in his/her true element, they become more productive, instill more value in the world and enjoy greater personal as well as professional fulfillment. And surprise surprise – they make more money!

What are the things that you've been good at always? What are the things that come to you with ease and you often wonder why others find it so challenging? Are you naturally creative and innovative to come up with out of the box ideas? Are you a genius where details are concerned, naturally executing projects that need precision? Are you a gifted communicator who doesn't have any difficulty in articulating or expressing yourself clearly? Are you a diplomat, negotiator, leader, solution-provider, good listen, networker, change agent, technocrat? What are your natural strengths?

Now, you may or may not be passionate about what you possess a natural talent for. A fine, agile and graceful dancer may not be passionate about dancing. Similarly, someone who has a knack for writing really well may not be a passionate writer. However, a majority of people do not show aspirations and ambitions towards things they aren't good at. You are less likely to be passionate about programming when you don't possess an inherent aptitude for technology. Get the drift?

Howard Thurmon put it across brilliantly when he said, "Don't ask yourself what the world needs; ask yourself what makes you come alive, then do that. Because what the world needs is people who have come alive."

2. How do you measure life?

If you don't stand for something, you'll fall for just about anything! How do you want your life to be measured? Measuring your life means taking a clear stand to stand for something and then aligning your existence to it.

Living with a strong purpose is focusing on things that matter the most to you. Having said that, something that matters most to you will rarely be "things!" While some folks have the liberty of swapping the security of a regular 9-5 job to chase their passion, others have short-term goals and responsibilities to take care of – thinking paying off debt, providing for their kids, paying bills and more. However, you don't really have to choose between money and passion all the time. Sometimes, a plain shift in the perspective and ideas can change your experiences.

Identifying your purpose pushes you to accept challenges and stretch you beyond your comfort zone to inspire you. A boat under pressure can manage a wave of any magnitude if it is placed perpendicular to it. Similarly, your perspective and purpose can help you tackle any challenge.

3. What brings you alive?

This is one important question that will get you thinking in the right direction when it comes to identifying your purpose. What is it that makes you come alive? What are the things that inspire you? What is it that lights up a fire in your belly? When I say what makes you come alive, I am not referring to your video games or favorite football team games or your fancy wardrobe (unless you are sports professional or stylist), I am referring to a purpose that's something bigger. It is about connecting at a deeper level with what you are passionate about? It is the awareness that when you are passionate about something and put your attention on it, you can increase your influence and positive impact in ways that few other things can. It is taking on endeavors that light a fire in your belly to make a difference.

Of course, you don't have to be the big-ticket inventor or find the cure for cancer (though why not?). This is about discovering a cause that is higher than you but is also in alignment with who you truly are as a person.

4. Where can you add the highest value?

Taking on something you are innately good at but hate doing is not the best route to fulfillment. However, knowing your inherent strengths and merging it with where you can add maximum value through the implementation of your knowledge, aptitude, education, skills, experience and more helps you concentrate on professional opportunities and roles where you have high chances of succeeding, while also awarding you a high sense of achievement, fulfillment, and contribution.

People tend to undervalue the abilities and skills that they have a natural expertise for. Try to reframe the concept of value addition by asking yourself "what problem can you help solve within your organization?" what are the problems that you are passionate about solving or that gives you a sense of fulfillment while solving? This way, you'll focus more on your inherent strengths and the things you are naturally good at than trying to overcome your weaknesses.

5. If money wasn't an issue, what would you do?

This is a good question to ask yourself for determining if you are being driven by money alone or also have passion to go along with it.

Money drives a good number of us. However, it may not always be the primary driver or purpose of your life. It can be just one of the many "whys" or a means to fulfill a "why." Your "why" may be to open a cancer treatment research institute or a charity which needs a good amount of money. Look at what you are currently doing and question yourself if you'd still do it if money was not a consideration. Would you? Be honest. If you had all the money in the world, would you still do what you are presently doing? High chances no! If your answer is no (which means you are a part of the majority), you are stuck in a job! I won't say get up now and become a professional athlete, a ballet dancer or a runway model – that's slightly unrealistic (though let no one define your parameters of realistic and unrealistic).

However, you need a career, not a job you are stuck in. a rewarding, fulfilling career that you love, and that drives you to get up each morning and head to work. When you are in a career you love, you'll give it your best shot, which will increase your chances of success and wealth. Again, if you are 9-5 bucket carrier, you can't quit everything overnight and run behind what you love doing. You'll begin with one step a time, climbing one rung after another to slowly make your way to the top. The "why" helps you wake up in the morning and give it your all. Unless you plug into your purpose and take action towards fulfilling that purpose, your chances of success are dim! When you plug into your "why," the how is never a challenge.

If you do something you are deeply passionate about, you boost your success chances. When you toil on something that lights up your fire, it stops seemingly like work. It is similar to building a dream, one task at a time. Pick something that you have a huge interest in. Combine this with external rewards, a sense of inner fulfillment and value addition, and you'll find your "why." You'll pour everything into it if you are driven by a deep passion and desire to do something. All successful people from Bill Gates to Steve Jobs were visionaries passionate about what they were doing.

If you do something merely for external rewards or money, it may not sustain in the long run. Sustained efforts will be a challenge after the initially euphoria fades. You'll probably quit and find other ways to make money. However, if you are guided by passion, your drive to keep going in the face of obstacles will help you stay on course. This is because the passion will bring a sense of fulfillment!

Having said that let me also reiterate that passion alone doesn't survive for long if it doesn't generate the required results. You may be passionate about writing poems. However, if it doesn't help you sustain financially or help you lead a decent life, it'll wither faster than you realize. This is exactly why your purpose or why has to be the sweet spot between intrinsic and extrinsic motivators.

6. What past signposts can I use to define your future?

Go back to your past to discover the getaway to your future. It may help you define your purpose. What made you tick as a child when there were no worldly considerations? What were the things you loved doing or derived pure joy out of during your childhood and teen years? Did you derive great joy from playing a particular sport? Or participating in dramas/theatre? How about playing a musical instrument, writing poems or painting? Drawing comic characters, playing video games or looking after animals?

I know most of you will want to hit me hard now and say, but we can't make money out of all these childhood passions when reality hits us? Why not? Idea and a game plan are the keys. I know many successful artists and painters who make a killing by auctioning their artworks. They employ slick marketing ideas and resourcefully tap into multiple channels to convert their passion into a financially rewarding profession. What stops a passionate horse rider from making a killing out of taking horse riding lessons for enthusiasts? What is stopping you from developing ideas into money-making opportunities? Your own inner, self-limiting beliefs! Passion and monetary rewards aren't mutually exclusive. You can have both. There are innumerable examples around you of people who love doing what they do, which in turn helps them make even more money. So next time, someone asks you, or you ask yourself –passion or financial rewards – say both!

Go back to your past for references on how you can shape your future. What are the things that you loved doing when money was not a criterion? You'll find some truly revealing answers!

A man came across three laborers who were busy laying bricks. He questioned the first bricklayer about what he was up to. "Can't you see I am laying bricks on the plot?" The man then asked the second laborer what he was doing, "I am building a wall," he replied. Finally, the passerby went to the third bricklayer and similarly questioned him about what he was doing. Pat came the reply, "I am building a church here."

Did you notice the three distinct perspectives? All three men were doing the exact same work yet the way they viewed their work or the purpose with which they were doing it differed. While one saw it a merely laying bricks on the plot, the other's purpose was to build a church. The first worker most likely was the one who was only concerned about his paycheck. He viewed his work as a task that had to be completed only for money. The first laborer wasn't too concerned about the outcome. He was the first one to run out once the end bell rang. The second laborer was probably driven by the need to complete his task and derive a sense of fulfillment from the completion of his task. he is the type who would put in some extra time and effort to see the task to its completion.

However, it was the third laborer who was driven by a desire to create a religious structure, which would bring divinity to the community and increase worship. There was a higher purpose to his work than simply getting his paycheck or completing the task. This higher purpose drove him to be the best at his job. Every brick that he laid was seen as a vision of grandiose, glory and aspiration. He was the type of worker who would do everything it takes to bring his vision to fulfillment.

Here are some questions you can ask yourself for figuring out your why if you haven't already found it by now.

1. Why do you do what you do?

2. What excites you about your present job or career?

3. What is your idea of a fantastic day?

4. What is success to you beyond your paycheck?

5. How does real success feel?

6. What do you desire to feel about your influence on the world once you retire?

7. What do you dislike about your present job or career?

8. Why aren't you doing something else?

9. What does a typical bad day look like?

10. What are the things you don't really enjoy about your work?

11. What is failure for you beyond the paycheck?

12. What does failure look like to you?

Other than knowing what you want, your purpose can also be defined by what you don't want. When you know what you don't want, you'll know what you are truly chasing, which helps define your purpose in life.

What are you intrinsic and extrinsic motivators?

Intrinsic motivation is behavior that is guided by internal rewards. In simple words, the motivation to do something originates from the individual because he/she feels an internally rewarded for it. There are three main types of intrinsic motivators according to Weinberg and Gould –knowledge, stimulation and accomplishment.

A person may do something for a genuine thirst of acquiring knowledge or learn more about a subject. Similarly, a person can feel motivated to do something to enjoy a sense of accomplishment or achievement. Stimulation or challenging/interesting tasks that drive us to do our best are also a form of intrinsic motivation. The rewards come from within us not outside of us, unlike extrinsic motivation.

Extrinsic motivation is behavior impacted by external rewards such as grades, fame, wealth and applause/praise. This originates from outside the individual in contrast to intrinsic motivation, which comes from within. Performance related rewards can drive an individual to action. To stay on the course of your goals, you need a healthy combination of both intrinsic and extrinsic motivation. You should be internally driven by a purpose and external driven by the rewards that come from fulfilling the goal. An inner sense of fulfillment and external rewards both are integral to the purpose of goal fulfillment.

Make a list of your intrinsic and extrinsic motivators before you head any further.

Remember, each person's definition of success is different because their "why" is different from yours. For someone, giving their family comfortable life can term them a success. For others, it can be the power and ability to touch other people's life selflessly that can be termed a success. Still, others may view going back to college and getting a degree as success. Your definition of success is a good indicator of your "why."

Chapter Two: Success Habit Two - Copycat Your Way to Success

Most things in life don't need to be reinvented. You probably need to improve an existing idea, concept or thought. Maybe find a way to do things differently to produce greater efficiency or results. However, there's no need to reinvent the wheel all the time.

Think about it, your time on earth is limited, and you have only so many years to be productive and build wealth. Why would you do something from scratch that eats up all your time when you can simply copy paste a system that is already working well for others. The smartest way to progress in today's world is to follow something that's already proven to be a success or emulate a proven model.

Start where they started not where they are currently

However, the success lies in details. Successfully duplicating a system is also an art. For instance, you can't model your business on someone who is 2000 steps ahead of you. If you are building a social network for travelers, you can't emulate what Facebook is doing now. You will have to go back to what Zuckerberg did when he launched Facebook. The correct approach would be to identify all the key points he implemented to help Facebook gain the right starter traction. Say, hyper-focusing on Harvard students, inducing a feeling of being a part of an exclusive community and developing a platform for like-minded individuals.

In short, take the core founding principle of a plan and apply them to your idea. In the above example, we use the basic founding principles of Facebook to build a social network exclusively for travelers. Get the idea, right? You have to judiciously pick what they did at the same stage or level as the one you are in currently.

Let's say you are a food delivery start-up that has four employees. Now, you don't model yourself around what a food delivery giant is currently doing with a 2000 plus employees. You emulate what they did when they started with four employees. How can you model a billionaire's current methods with $200 in your pocket? You've got to adopt the methods he/she adopted to become a billionaire when they had $200.

Keep in mind changing trends

The principles of technology, doing business and buying may not be the same today as they were a few decades or years ago. Factor in time, changing trends and a shift in the way business is done too. For instance, a few years ago, e-commerce retailers relied solely on computers for generating sales. Today, if you ignore smartphone and tab users, you'll leave a lot of money on the table for competitors.

If you want to emulate a business, look at the principles on which it is based rather than exactly how they accomplished something.

Things change dynamically in today's era. To keep up with the fast-paced, action-packed business world, look for the wider principles than the exact technique. However, if you can find success using the exact, what's to stop you from using it?

Why Not Create My Own Unique Method

You may wonder about why one shouldn't create his/her own unique methods and systems. If you are in the business of invention, then yes, by all means, create your own methods and systems through trial and error. However, if you are aiming to make a success in a field that is already established, there is no need to reinvent the wheel or spend time, money and effort trying to find a different way to do things (when the current method is clearly working).

Identify what is effective for others, copycat it smartly and add your own unique twist to then recreate a different and better model. You need ideas to spark yours, an already established working process to emulate. Think about corporations such as Apple. It certainly wasn't the first to invent its line of products. They were ingenious enough to innovate upon things that were already in place.

Smart entrepreneurs are smarter copycats! They don't wasn't time creating every single spoke of the wheel or every aspect of their business model. They are astute innovators, not time-consuming inventors. Most big organizations rose to their glory through innovation and imitation.

Why do you think internet marketers are making a fortune selling their secret, money making strategies online? They make more money teaching about these strategies than they probably make from their online business. Logically, if they were making more from the business, wouldn't they just be keeping these secrets to themselves rather than invite more competition? This is because there is a huge demand of copycat systems in the online and offline world today. People want to invest their money, time and energy on things that are already proven to work.

Building something from scratch takes plenty of time, money and effort and offers tiny results. Time is precious. You spend a huge amount of time trying to build a business only to realize that you've spent your time on a turkey or yielded little results that are just not worth it. Tweak what's in place and own it like a boss! That's the smart way to do business today. Think about productivity and efficiency- think in terms of creating big results over a shorter span of time to make the most of your time, effort and money investment. Effective enterprises make huge money in a relatively shorter span of time. Instead of finding new systems and testing technological platforms, find a successful business in your field and copy the system they use. They are obviously acing it!

Here are a few ideas to copycat your way to success.

1. Find a business leader in your industry.

Identify a person who is successful in a business similar to yours or one you aspire to get into. If you are witnessing slow growth in any aspect of the business, a smart thing to do would be to identify who is successful or a leader in the exact same business area and copy their method! For example, if you are performing well with customer retention. However, the business falters when it comes to new customer acquisition, identify a business in your industry that does soaringly well when it comes to acquiring new customers. Next, copy their customer acquisition methods (maybe add your own innovative twists).

2. Aim to closer to the industry leader

Study the business leader carefully by getting as much into their inner circle as possible. Opt-in to their leader's list. Sign up for their newsletters. Stalk them on their social media to see what type of posts garner maximum reactions. Observe what gets their audience to engage, converse and take action. Try and establish a rapport with the founder, thought leader or influencer of the business. Attend seminars conducted by them or where you can bump into them. Follow them on social Facebook, LinkedIn, and Twitter. Network your way into their inner circle.

One of the best ways to do it is by consistently leaving insightful comments on their blogs and social media posts. When you leave valuable comments on someone's posts or contribute to the discussion insightfully, people take note. Sooner or later, the leader will notice you. Add value and keep helping others to get these thought leaders to notice and help you when you need collaboration, suggestions, and advice. Thought leaders are naturally drawn to other insightful and knowledgeable thinkers who present path-breaking ideas and solutions.

Another super tip for approaching thought leaders is to email them and tell them why you admire them. Don't ask for any favors or suggestions. Simply mention one or two specific reasons why you admire them. For instance, "I truly appreciate the way to bring strategic, out of the box employee retention solutions" or "your views on mergers and acquisitions were unusual and well-thought." Don't pay vague compliments like "I really love your blog" or "I am a fan of your writing and views." Being specific is the key. Don't come across as desperate when you mail them. I'd all recommend using their products or services and sharing your reviews/feedback about the same.

3. Observe how he/she does business

Stalk (well not literally) your business leader to learn how they do business and why. Identify and single out their best practices. Watch how they conduct their business. When you learn how the masters do it, why do it any other way? How does the person operate his/her business? What are the various aspects of their business? Understand their business and monetization model. Pick up one or two things from their operation to accelerate your business. For instance, you may observe that the top performers and company founders are almost always engaged in giving presentations to clients for boosting their results, while they've hired support staff for time-consuming activities such as sending across emails on their behalf to prospective clients. You realize delegation leverages time, efforts and skills. Follow suit and employ the same strategies for your business.

In today's world, it is easy to understand a business model because everything is online. Study the business thoroughly online to know their inner workings. Does the business have an online presence? How are their landing pages, blogs, and websites designed? How are their emails and social media posts written? How is their sales copy drafted? How are their blogs written? How does the owner/founder/staff interact with followers on social media channels? How do they launch their products? How do they build hype before, during and post the launch?

Copycat business leaders Start applying your business mentor's most effective practices to your business, one small step at a time. Several internet and offline business have found huge success by emulating and innovating upon the systems of other successful enterprises. Of course, hard work cannot be discounted. However, today it is also about smart work strategies. And one of the smartest things you can do to skyrocket your way to wealth and success is to follow established money-making systems.

If you think the packaging of a product is hugely attractive for customers, why opt for any other colors? Similarly, if a font and image placement is working wonderfully for a book cover design, why experiment with something else. There have been successful people before you who've already done the hard work by experimenting. Save yourself the sweat and simply copycat your way to success by following what's proven to work.

4. Keep track of everything that inspires you

A smart copycat always has a scrapbook filled with ideas. There are plenty of apps notes features you can use on your smartphone or tab for the idea creation or note-taking process. Notice any successful, visionary with plenty of ideas. Their books and apps are always full of sketches, pictures, stories, one world clues, and roughly written ideas.

This way when you come across an idea that you can use for your own business, you can quickly note it down for future reference. Ideas are often lost when they are not committed to a document because our hyperactive brain can only remember so much. Get into the habit of recording your ideas, and systems you wish to emulate. It can be anything from a new word or phrase used by a competitor that can be used in your own copy or a system a business is using to cut down their operational costs.

At times, someone else ideas will inspire and drive you to build your own ideas around it. Our own ideas come from a combination of different ideas, which were created by other leaders in rough bits.

5. Copy ideas and concepts

Unless there's a clear intellectual copyright law or legislation in your region that I am not aware of, thankfully there is nothing that stops you from borrowing other people's ideas. Let us consider an example, say you want to be a huge success in the self-publishing industry. Now, you notice a successful eBook author make a killing by self-publishing books on Kindle.

You obviously can't copy what they write since it is copyright protected. However, there are ideas and concepts that you can borrow from to witness the same success the best-selling author does. So, you notice that the author not only creates eBooks but also audio versions and speeches out of it. This is the main formula for their success. Or they probably offer bundled version books to give greater value to their readers. There's nothing stopping you from using their success formula! So, while you can't in essence copy everything, you can borrow successful ideas, formulas, concepts, and strategies to your own work or business.

As a copycat, it is extremely important to abide by laws and basic courtesy. Be respectful of other people's work. Give credit wherever due. Don't do anything to others that you wouldn't want anyone to do to you. Be mindful of copyright and other laws before simply copy-pasting someone's system or ideas. Look around you, and you'll find copycats everywhere. FedEx borrowed from US Postal Service and came up with their own flat rate ship. Is it a new idea? If you watched CNBC's The Costo Craze, Inside the Warehouse Giant, you'll known what I am talking about. Costco sent their employees into the competitor's stores for tracking and sending product and pricing details to the company head office. They smartly termed it market research, when it was nothing more than copycatting! Don't pressurize yourself into creating new ideas all the time. Originality is at times slightly overhyped unless you come up with something truly revolutionary and path-breaking. Instead, step out and look for winning ideas that you can copy or improve upon.

In the above example, write your own winning eBook on a topic that works but give it your own unique twist. For instance, if you realize that books on how to enjoy a happy marriage work well, you can lend it your own angle with how to rebuild trust and enjoy a happy marriage after infidelity. You are lifting an already established and proven topic but also adding your own unique angle to define your readers. The ribs and bones are all there, just add the body. The hamburger is ready; enjoy it with your own original sauce. Get the idea?

6. Form beneficial associations

Mutually beneficial collaborations and partnerships are a great way to grow your business in the long run. You may have a social media page or community for mothers or travelers. How can you monetize now? Maybe approach other similar communities together combine forces to approach mom-baby or travel brands for advertising with a larger following. Similarly, a business can benefit from something you have, like a bigger audience while you can cash in on their subject matter expertise. It's a win-win situation, while also helping both the businesses save precious money, time and effort.

Chapter Three: Success Habit Three - Get a Mentor

"That said, I should also add that I learned a great deal from being allowed in these privileged circles and am grateful for the opportunity to have worked closely with some of the most powerful and successful people in the business including Steven Spielberg and Ted Turner." — Douglas Wood

Do you wonder how people acquired knowledge before Google, universities or even books? They learned from other people. Approaching and learning from other people has become even easier now with the advent of the internet and social media. Influencers, business heads, and thought leaders are more approachable and open to interacting with their audience than ever before. Mentorship dates back to the ancient Greek era when philosophers had their own disciplines that they passed down all their knowledge and wisdom to. It's a tried and tested method of learning from the experience, wisdom, and strategies of the seasoned players in the market.

Getting a solid, experienced and knowledgeable mentor can speed by your success meter 10 times faster. Don't know the best practices for getting a mentor? I am spilling all the beans here!

1. Never ask directly

The stupidest thing someone has ever done is approached me with emails asking if I'd be their mentor. A big no! Never approach leaders you fancy with emails urging them to be your mentor. They'll think you are being grossly delusional. Most people are helpful and don't mind pitching in when you need guidance or suggestion, but they aren't going to be joined at the hip with you. So, the word mentor is probably going to send them scooting in another direction.

Plus, help isn't a one-way street. If people go out of the way to do something for you, they'll expect you to return the favor too. There are no free lunches in the world! Keep your communication short, to the point and simple. You can ask them one or two questions or pay them a specific compliment (as discussed in the above chapter). Avoid asking for a huge favor at the onset.

When someone is offering you a huge value, don't undermine it by offering to buy them coffee or something silly to that effect. You have to be compelling enough to deserve someone's time and attention.

I've tried multiple approaches when it comes to approaching mentors, the one that works effectively for me is, offering a specific compliment to the thought leader mentor, followed by my own take on something they've recently blogged about, and finally ending with a question that I need more guidance on. Almost always works! You've satisfied their ego by telling them you admire their work and then revealed your knowledge/intelligence by offering your own unique take on a topic they recently discussed. Finally giving them the ultimate importance by seeking their valuable inputs on a problem, issue or topic! Who doesn't like it when people seek their guidance and suggestions?

There are tons of discussion threads and communities on LinkedIn, which is a goldmine for mentors. Find a threat or community that is relevant to your business/industry, look for active thoughts leaders and mentors who are regular conversations starters, add value to the discussions initiated by them. This is how you build your presence. You don't just ask someone for something, you earn your place as their mentee!

Say you are looking for a job and you meet someone influential within an industry where you want to establish yourself. You are introduced to the person at a networking event/seminar. What do you do next? Ask them for a job? You'll come across as a complete loser! Instead, how about asking them for a small favor (scanning your CV for any suggestions or feedback before you send it out to prospective employers)?

This way you'll cleverly present your entire skill set to them, while also staying on top of their mind when a similar role comes up. They may know someone who could use your skills or may contact you for a position in their /their references' organization. You didn't directly ask the influencer for a job but still made inroads into the world of opportunity within their organization or industry. Being smart and resourceful is the key.

Also, people really feel good when you ask them to share their two cents about something. So, you are serving a dual purpose by asking highly placed mentors to review your resume.

2. Spending time with doers increases our own 'doing' energy

Research has proven that we become most like the five people we spend maximum time with. Obviously, when you spend time with people, whether we like it or not, we end up taking on their energy at a subconscious level. It happens so subtly and unknowingly that you don't even realize. Thus, if you spend more time with people bogged down by inertia, procrastination, laziness, negativity, etc. you start thinking and feeling like them.

Instead, choose the people you spend maximum time with. Hobnob with the successful and wealthy to acquire their dynamic energy, mindset, and actions. Be with people who discuss ideas and solutions rather than problems. Ask yourself if interacting with a person adds value to the pursuit of being successful and wealthy? Do they contribute to your overall growth?

I'd like you to do a small experiment next time you are with a mixed group of people or at an office party. Interact with a high-performing or successful group of people and a not so well performing or average performing group of people. The former group's talks will be very different from the latter.

While performers always take in terms of their next action, ideas or solutions, average performers will be busy blaming the system, other people and circumstances for their inaction. They will have a more reactive than proactive approach. Their talks will be centered on excuses and problems, not solutions and ideas!

You'll quickly learn to tell the difference between these two groups and try to stick around with successful people once you observe how it impacts your own thoughts, actions, mindset, and habits.

Most successful and wealthy people didn't become wealthy and successful overnight. They transformed their life by bringing about a transformation within their mindset. Before they could acquire wealth and success in person, they started thinking rich and successful. When you mingle with these rich and successful people, you develop the same winning, ideas and solution-providing mindset.

3. Stay in touch

Don't expect to receive a reply with a single email or social media comment. When you approach people directly to be your mentor, there are different ways to do it. You probably met them at a networking event and don't want them to forget you, in which case you can send them a message or email saying it was wonderful meeting them and you'd like to stay in touch with them for future associations/collaborations.

Drop messages on holidays and festivals, so you still remain in their awareness. Sometimes, when you ask for something, they may not respond or may reply in the negative, stating they are busy. Accept it graciously and tell them you understand. Try sending them sending them information or links that are relevant and interesting to them in future. Exchanging emails on book recommendations, blogs, newspaper articles and questions is a good way to stay connected with your mentors.

You may not meet these people frequently. However, gently ask for their suggestions, and apply it. Give time for the relationship to build. However, keep the momentum going by staying in touch with them regularly. If they offer you a suggestion, advice or recommendation that worked, don forget it to drop them a mail mentioning it. The mentors will be even more encouraged to offer their advice, suggestions, and recommendations to people who truly appreciate it.

Create smart reasons to follow up with the person for maintaining the connection and relationship on a continual basis. If you discussed a specific topic with them during your face to face meeting, send them blogs or articles related to it with a note about how you enjoyed discussing the subject with them and thought they may find the blog/article interesting or valuable. Add references or bits from the conversation you both shared.

Never forget to send a thank you note if they do you a favor or offer you valuable advice/suggestions/recommendations. If something the mentors told you worked wonderfully well, don't forget to mention it to them. Keep coming up with reasons and opportunities to stay connected. There's no point in building your network without trying to stay in touch regularly.

4. Be serious about your craft

When you approach someone, who is highly successful in their field, there are high chances they take their craft very seriously. Successful and highly placed people look down upon energy wasters and time killers. You've got to prove that you take your craft seriously for them to take you seriously. Maintain the same intensity, passion, energy, and zeal for work as them. Show them how you are prepared to go the extra mile just to learn from them. Push the envelope. Let your infectious energy and enthusiasm rub off on others.

5. Avoid being a passive mentee

I know people who think they've attained the world's success once they latch on to a mentor. It doesn't work that way. You aren't a passive learner. You are in charge of your goals, nurturing a relationship with your mentor, actively seeking their advice and attending events whenever you get the opportunity.

Your efforts shouldn't end once you get a mentor. Building a fabulous network of mentors requires commitment, time and energy. At times, you'll have to travel to faraway places just to meet someone you've always admired from an industry once. Know yourself, your values and your working style to get maximum value from your relationship with the mentor.

6. Find someone who fills your skillset gaps

Don't chase a mentor who is your clone. Of course, you want to find someone whose ideologies, values and working style matches your own. However, find someone who can make up for the gaps in your skills. There's value in making your strengths even stronger, but there's greater value when someone can offer you guidance and advice in an area you are clearly struggling. Someone who can complement your skills makes for a great mentor.

Building success and wealth is about being in a constant state of learning and having the right people around you to accelerate the process of learning. It is important for the mentor to supplement your own strengths.

For instance, you may be a wonderful app designer who designs the slickest applications with the required technological finesse. However, you may lack the marketing acumen to promote these applications to users. A good mentor is someone who can step in and fill the gap to help you generate better marketing and promotion ideas.

7. Avoid following a mentor blindly

Understand that no one can live your life. Mentors are there to offer you advice, suggestions, and perspectives based on their experience. However, these may not be suitable for you or may need some tweaking, or you may need to build upon their ideas. Mentors can't make sweeping or unilateral decisions for you.

They can only offer suggestions. Whether to apply these suggestions and recommendations to your business/work should be your decision and discretion. A mentor's role is more to help you reflect upon something not follow it blindly.

8. Take time to make genuine connections

Don't pretend to be a social butterfly hopping from one group to another, giving the impression that you know a lot of people. It is the quality of your connections that matter, not the quantity. Take time out to make genuine connections with each person. Explore how you can add value to what they are doing and how you can benefit from their expertise and experience. Don't rush from one person to another in a bid to acquire plenty of business cards. However, spending half an hour with a good contact is more valuable than spending 2-3 minutes with 10 contacts.

You'll make the most of your networking opportunities by laser focusing on genuine contacts. Identify a handful of leaders, mentors, and contacts, and focus on them rather than acquiring a bagful of meaningless business cards, where people don't even recall having met you. Take time to figure out how you and the leader/mentor can add value to each other's projects or business. If you give them a solid value proposition, they'll be likely to associate with you in some manner or another.

Building connections is about nurturing relationships. Don't forget to thank your mentors, influencers or thought leaders for their suggestions, information or help. Keep notes about what was discussed in your last interaction with them so you can floor them by referencing the previous conversation. This adds a personalized touch to the correspondence.

9. Try and be a part of as many professional groups as possible

Be a part of maximum online and offline professional groups, organizations, business bodies and clubs where people from your industry are most likely to hang out. These are great places to bump into like-minded people who you can learn from or collaborate with in future. Don't miss business networking events, seminars, conferences, talks, exhibitions, and lunches within your city or industry. These are the best places to meet people from your field.

One pro tip I can offer you for making a positive impression on people is volunteering. Take up additional responsibilities within your organization /outside the organization or offer to help the mentor by going beyond your call of duty. This is a great way to gain people's attention and increase your visibility. When there is suitable opportunity for a tie-up, association or job, your proactive disposition will boost your chances of being considered over others. Try and seek tips from experts about expanding your network.

10. Leverage the power of your social contacts by asking for references

Remember the six degrees of separation rule? It states that every person on the planet can be connected to another person through a link comprising a maximum of five acquaintances or contacts. It means you are closer to your mentor than you think. You simply have to exploit the power of your existing contact list to build more contacts or acquire a mentor. Meeting people through contacts you already know saves you the trouble of approaching your mentor as a stranger. If you want to be introduced to a big leader or mentor within the industry, hang around with folks who know him/her for a while.

Don't ask for their contact details or request an appointment immediately. Make a polite request to be introduced to the biggie. Look out for the introduction feature on LinkedIn, where existing contacts can introduce you to new professional acquaintances.

When you spot a large group at a business networking event and know a few people from the group, walk over and greet the people you know, while introducing yourself to new acquaintances. Exchange business cards and try to get everyone's contact details. Of course, this isn't the place to ask for a job, association, mentorship, business or any favors. Instead, ask for the person's suggestions, advice or recommendations.

Remember, you are leveraging these contacts for future, which means immediate favors are huge no-no. For instance, if you are looking for a job, you can't ask someone for job straightaway. Instead, you can seek their counsel on tips that can help your job search. This presents you as less desperate, and more credible professional.

The primary objective while networking with people before you approach a mentor should be to build rapport and develop sustainable, long-term professional associations. Don't look for quick, short-term gains when it comes to building relationships with mentors or influential people within your industry.

Keep asking your existing contacts for references or introductions. Each person you know in turn knows around 200 people. Don't leave a valuable network source untapped. One of the fastest ways to grow your network is to request existing contacts for recommendations. They'll be even happier to share names from their contact list if you share some from yours. It's a 'you scratch my back, I scratch yours' world.

11. Listen, buddy,

When you talk, you only reinforce what you already know. However, when you listen, you learn something new. Avoid doing all the talking to impress a prospective mentor and listen. Ask for the other person's advice, opinion and take on an important issue within the industry.

Let them add value to your knowledge. If you keep talking, the other person gets the impression that you aren't interested in what they are speaking. Also, offer verbal and non-acknowledgments that you are keenly listening to them. Verbal clues can be "aha," "ohh" and "hmm," while nonverbal listening clues can be nodding your head. You can also paraphrase what the other person said to demonstrate you've been actively listening to them. I also like to ask the person questions about what he/she said not just to check my understanding but also cleverly signal to the other person that I've been keenly listening to them. We often fail to realize that our listening skills impress people as much as our speaking skills. You can pose insight questions about something they've said to floor them.

Tips for approaching influencers and thought leaders on social media and other online platforms

1. Research and more research. There are multiple tools such as Buzzsumo (with its power-packed influencer suite) that lets you not just discover but also reach out to and study influencer data. They have a handy search engine

that allows people to find the most powerful influencers in any topic/industry. There are additional features as well that assist with your outreach plan. Another handy application that allows you to identify social media influencers and monitor conversations is Hootsuite. You can build and save a Twitter list on the platform to easily track your influencer and engagement details. How cool is that?

2. Join online chats your target influencer is especially active in. There are plenty of conversations happening within online platforms and if you are trying to pursue a relationship with the intended influencer, and then participate actively in the conversations. Find the most active conversations and experts on Reddit, Quora, LinkedIn Groups and other niche webinars. Identify where your influencers hangout and start making your presence felt on these platforms. Twitter is a good place to begin impressing influencers within your industry. Organized by a hashtag, there are plenty of conversations happening in the online world.

Find ones that are relevant to your industry or area of expertise and slay it!

3. Tap mutual contacts This isn't the most earth-shattering strategy, but it's often the basics we ignore. Look for any mutual connections between you and the influencer. The world is smaller than we believe. Approach your own social media contact of follower and request them to introduce you to the influencer. This way they aren't caught off-guard.

4. Keep it organized. If you are reaching out to plenty of influencers in the hope that one of them agrees to mentor you, keep it organized. Keep tabs of the dates you approached them, the conversations you had, the date/time they asked you to get back to them and more. This way you are likely to impress these influencers with your diligence and disciplined efforts. Plus, you'll avoid plenty of awkward situations.

5. Try MicroMentor or SCORE Mentoring. These two are online platforms that provide small business owners and newbies access to a mentor.

You can find plenty of mentors here or even volunteer to be one yourself. SCORE Mentoring has volunteers having expertise across 62 industries so there's every chance you may find someone who knows your industry in and out. Leverage the power of these platforms to find your mentors online.

How to find and retain a mentor – the steps

Most people do not understand the concept on mentoring, and that includes me in my initial days as well. We often think that mentoring is about us, and about finding the best mentor/teacher! Nope, you need someone who not only knows their craft well but also someone who will invest in you and teach you. And finally – You've got to get the job done, the mentor will only lead you to it! Here are my secret steps to not get an awesome mentor but also keep him/her.

1. Look for someone you want to emulate. Don't just go mentoring hunting and grab the first duck you find. You don't only need someone who is

rich, successful and good at their work. You also want someone whose values, work style and outlook match yours. Who do you aspire to be like? Find someone you admire, like and can identify with. Take your time to scan several candidates before you zero down on your mentor who is most like the person you want to be a few years down the line.

2. Research the person. Once you've identified a mentor or couple of mentors, know them thoroughly. Follow their blogs and social media accounts. Do you like their public persona? Ensure you understand their strengths and limitations. Keep realistic expectations.

3. Schedule a meeting. Like we discussed earlier, don't ask the person to be your mentor. Instead, prepare a list of questions but don't fish it out in front of the mentor. Use it to guide your conversations, which should flow organically. Adapt to the mentor's communication style. If he/she is being more formal, adopt a similar approach. However, don't fall into the trap of

acting like old buddies if he/she acts uber cool and casual. Avoid taking liberties with your mentor, and maintain the mentor-mentee equation throughout.

Rather than requesting for a formal meeting, ask to talk to your mentor over coffee or brunch. Keep it less than a couple of hours. The first meeting should be crisp, and to the point so they look forward to meeting you again. Stretch it too much, and you'll send them running.

4. Evaluate the interaction. Once you meet this person, ask yourself if you want to spend more time interacting with them. How are their vibes? Do they make you feel positive, inspired and encouraged to reach your goals? Did they ask you enough questions and the right ones? Did they provide you with answers to questions you posed? Did you feel a connection with them? Do you think the relationship can continue over a period of time? If it is mostly yes, create a follow-up plan.

5. Follow up. Okay now, this isn't like dating. You can appear eager and overambitious. In fact, you should show an extra zeal to be someone's mentee. Just don't come across as too desperate though. There's a fine line between the two. Follow up by thanking the mentor for their time, patience and insights. You can send an email or text without coming across as overbearing.

Seize this opportunity to mention that you'd like to meet them again. If he/she agrees, grab a calendar and fix a date-time immediately if you can. Ensure the mentor is relaxed and doesn't feel pressurized to give in to your request.

6. Let the relationship build naturally. Don't place too many expectations on mentoring or force relationship-building. Allow it to evolve naturally over a period of time. It is pretty much like any other relationship, based on mutual trust, loyalty, and respect. Give it time to flourish. Forcing the relationship will only kill an otherwise wonderful relationship.

Chapter Four: Success Habit Four - Be Proactive Not Reactive

A young couple was once making dinner preparations. The lady cut off the edges of the ham before putting it in a baking pan. Her husband questioned her about why she did because it seemed like such as waste.

The lady replied. "I really don't know." I cut off the edges of the ham before baking it because that is what I saw my mom doing."

The couple then approached the lady's mother and questioned her about why she cut off the edges of the ham before she basked it. "I wouldn't know. My mother always did that, and I followed suit."

Next, they go to the lady's grandmother and ask her why she always cut off the ends of the ham before baking it. Pat came the reply, "that was really the only way I could fit the ham in my small pan."

This is pretty much what most people do in their life. They live their life on autopilot, doing what other people do without taking control of their life or knowing why they do what they do. Sleepwalking through life won't get you anywhere. We barely stop to ponder over why we do what we do. We simply react to whatever comes our way instead of being courageous enough to build our own path. There are multiple choices available to us and in our limited, reactive perspective of things; we fail to see the bigger picture.

Don't do what others did with their 'pan.' You have your own, unique 'pan.' Be proactive enough to determine how and why you do something.

Let me be crystal clear here – you are seldom going to build a wealthy, successful and fulfilling life by adopting a reactive approach. Reactive people are guided by their external circumstances, other people and things outside their control, which means if you hold a reactive approach you are limiting your chances of success. If your company is on a mass lay-off drive to cut costs and you lose your job, there that's the end of the world for you. Reactive people respond to circumstances and other things beyond their control, while proactive people accept the responsibility for their actions, irrespective of their circumstances, people and other factors that are beyond their control. They hold the steering wheel of their life and take it where they want to, never mind the road bumps and obstacles around them.

Rather than offering excuses or blaming people or waiting for opportunity to knock on their door, they go out and create doors! Proactive people will accept responsibility for their actions, and hold themselves accountable for everything they do. You either have a reason to succeed, where you succeed despite all obstacles or you have an excuse to not succeed, where you fail despite being offered several opportunities. You can't have both. Reactive people have excuses, while proactive people have compelling reasons to succeed (their whys).

Accept what is beyond your control and work on what it. There are some things that will be beyond your control however much you desire to change them. Your race, skin color, ethnicity, family background, growing up circumstances, height, birthplace or place you were raised and others. These are a few examples of factors that are beyond your control. You just can't do anything about it. All you can control is how you react to it. You can either whine about the fact that you were born in an underprivileged and racial set-up or you can convert your supposed weaknesses into strengths and go on to become a high on empathy champ from people from different walks of life by being the highest paid television show host – think Oprah Winfrey. Successful people realize pretty early on that they are in charge of their life, and that the key to unlocking their dream destiny is in their hands.

I know a few of you are thinking, I know it is great to proactive, but I am struggling to develop a proactive mindset. Fret not, like other success strategies and principles; I've got you covered here too. Here are some of my best tips to develop a more proactive approach.

1. Focus on solutions, not problems

A major difference between proactive and reactive people is that while reactive people are focused on problems, proactive folks are solution centric. They choose to focus on the solution instead of obsessing over a problem. Every run into challenges and circumstances that are beyond their control! However, how to tackle these obstacles is how distinguishes a winner from a loser! Forget about what is outside your realm of control, and instead focus on what you can do.

In the above lay-off example, you can't control global recession and increasing operational costs. However, you can control how you choose to use the time you have at hand once you're laid off.

You can go back to college, learn a course to upgrade your skills, take up a part-time job while studying, build an online business from home or do several other similar things. This is a proactive approach. A reactive or victim approach would be, "I've been laid off or been hit by tough market conditions. I can't do anything about it but wait for another job. This is my wretched destiny." See the difference? Proactive people will never play victims. They will have a more dynamic, broader and solution-oriented view of life.

Learn to won your challenges instead of blaming other people or circumstances for it. You alone are responsible for accomplishing your goals and fixing your problems. While plenty of people will support and nurture you, you alone are responsible for your success or failure. Take ownership of the challenges in your life, and convert them into opportunities. Work towards resolving your issues instead of blaming others.

2. Build your own luck

You can't sleep until the right opportunity comes your way. You have to go out there and create your own opportunities. How about taking a few steps each day to be better than what you were the previous day while moving ahead in a progressive, positive trajectory.

Make a blueprint on paper about where you want to be. Chalk out milestones for yourself with precise timelines. Things do not just happen because you desperately want them to happen. They happen when you make them happen.

3. Anticipate for the future and have your plan ready

Proactive people don't just sit there waiting to be washed away by the rain. They will be ready with their umbrellas. Develop a more proactive approach towards life by anticipating the future and preparing for it well in advance. By considering potential issues which may arise in future, you can plan for it well in advance. Let us say you have planned a vacation a few months from now. You start putting aside funds for the vacation by cutting down on eating outside and instead opting for home-cooked meals or opting for coffee at the vending machine rather than purchasing it at cafes.

This helps you take care of your food, travel and activity expenses during the destination. A reactive approach would be to plan activities, food and other expenses depending on the amount you are left with during the time of your vacation. The first point to work on for developing a proactive approach is to anticipate the future and prepare for it.

People with a proactive mindset have great foresight. They are seldom caught by surprise or are unprepared for any issue. Understand how everything around you works. Observe patterns, identify regular routines and anticipate the unexpected. What are the daily practices in your job or business? What are its natural cycles? What are the unexpected factors that can impact your business or work? All the same, don't be restricted by the past when it comes to making predictions or anticipating the future. Use your imagination to anticipate future outcomes. Use a combination of logic, resourcefulness, and creativity. Come up with several scenarios of how events can unfold in future. Some of the most proactive folks I know are forever on their feet – anticipating, thinking, planning and executing. They are hustlers who don't believe in lying low or becoming complacent.

3. Participate instead of being a passive audience

Be a part of as many opportunities, responsibilities and initiatives as possible without burning yourself out. If there's additional responsibility to taken at your workplace, proactively volunteer for it! Be a part of community initiatives, competitions, and events. Don't be a passive audience who simply watches others do their thing. Get up, go out there and make yourself visible. This is the only way to bring more opportunities your way, instead of sitting and waiting for them to happen!

I know plenty of people who just sit through meetings without adding any value or their own inputs, and then wonder why they don't get promoted. Add your own inputs to meetings and contribute to add value to any professional endeavor. Don't simply listen or react to other people's suggestions, throw in yours. Watching from the sidelines isn't the best thing to do if you want to develop a more proactive approach.

4. Avoid jumping to negative conclusions and manage your reactions

It is easy to succumb to emotional impulses or make snap judgments. Proactive people seldom engage in catastrophic thinking or giving in to their emotions. Gather all the information you can before arriving at a conclusion. Maintain a broader and open outlook to think logically and come up with more balanced solutions.

So, you texted someone, and they didn't reply. Do not automatically assume that he/she is avoiding you or deliberately not answering your calls. Think more balanced or realistic thoughts such they must be busy, driving or must not have their phone with them at the moment. There can be innumerable possibilities. Instead of imagining the worst, think of more realistic possibilities. This is another super tip for building a proactive approach.

Being proactive requires you to place yourself in the other person's shoe to understand things from their perspective. This prevents you from seeing things solely from your perspective and lends you the ability to try and come up with a solution.

5. Surround yourself with the right people

Surrounding yourself with positive, hard-working, inspiring and proactive people is one of the best ways to develop a winner's mindset. Spend your time and energy on people who are driven. You cannot spend a huge chunk of your time on reactive people who play victims and expect to demonstrate a more proactive approach. Avoid lazy, de-motivated and negative people like the plague. They'll pull your down with their negative mindset, and you'll be consumed by their inertia before you realize.

6. Take stock of your tasks

Being proactive is about being organized. This can include everything from your mindset to your physical workspace to your schedule. Proactively organizing your tasks allows for the tasks to be completed more efficiently, and gives you greater time for exploring opportunities. Lead a balanced life, schedule a downtime for leisure and maintain an overall positive outlook in life. Take stock of your responsibilities. Always be the employee, worker or businessman is willing to go the extra mile. A ready and willing attitude makes you more proactive. You'll be seen as someone who can be counted upon. Here is a list of questions you can ask yourself for developing a more proactive mindset.

1. What are your long-term and immediate tasks/goals?

2. What are your current priorities?

3. What tasks can you consolidate, shorten or discard altogether?

4. How can you stay ahead of tasks that aren't urgent?

5. What are the things you need to learn to be exceptionally good in your work?

6. What is your approach towards solving problems?

7. Can you foresee problems and plan alternatives and solutions in anticipation to these problems?

8. Can you automate tasks to make yourself more effective and save time?

As a proactive person, learn to get things done. Hold yourself accountable to complete a task. Make sure you accomplish something in the designated time. One of the best ways to increase your accountability to the goal or task is to enlist the help of an accountability buddy. This person is someone you can trust and who holds you accountable for your actions, while constantly reminding you of your goals.

Another way that works wonderfully well for some is to start writing and accountability blog or posting on social media. When you publicly commit to a goal or task, there are higher chances of you fulfilling you because you obviously don't want to be seen as a person who doesn't keep their word or is too lazy to work on what you commit to. Track your progress through your blog. This will not only help you stay on the course of your goals but also become a journey to inspire others.

7. The more you do, the more you learn. I'd love to tell you that the secret to being a wealthy and successful person is only reading or listening to eBooks like these. Unfortunately, that's not the way it works. You can acquire all the knowledge and inspiration in the world, but it is pointless if you don't implement it. Knowledge gains power only when put into action. Proactive people don't just read, watch and hear inspirational stuff to sit

and hatch eggs. They push themselves to apply the knowledge they acquire by promptly acting upon it. For them, failure is preferred over inaction.

When proactive people fail, they learn one more way not to do something or realize that they need to change or rethink their strategy. Let u say you build your own Facebook parenting blog/page and keep posting awesome on it. I mean, at least you think you are posting phenomenal content. You aggressively promote your blog to laser target a suitable audience group (think parents) using contests and inviting friends to like your page. However, even though you've built a fairly impressive following in a short span of time, the blog doesn't boast of great engagement in terms of likes, comments, user posts, and conversations.

You realize that though you managed to get plenty of followers onboard quickly owing to the contests and friend invitations, you didn't draw a keenly interested bunch of audience, which led to low engagement. People probably followed the blog only to win a few prizes or because they felt obliged to because they were your friends. This leads to the realization that you need an audience who is keenly interested in your blog. Thus, you start hyper-targeting your audience with Facebook Advertising. Why am I telling you all this? How on earth would you know what works and what doesn't if you don't take action? All successful and wealthy people who've accomplished life mastery took action in the direction of their dreams. They tried, failed, tweaked, reinvented, duplicated and so on. However, they could do all this only because they were proactive enough to implement the gathered knowledge.

How would you know what worked or didn't work for a parenting blog if you didn't start one in the first place! Yes, there are other systems to duplicate but some insider lessons you will have to learn on your own. No one's going to share all their secret success strategies with you. Not even the best of mentors. It is your unique journey, which needs to be lived and defined by you alone by demonstrating a more proactive approach. There are systems in place, but you'll have to lend it your own twist based on your unique approach, goals, and ideals.

In the above example, if you had simply read about building a Facebook blog and not acted upon it in the fear of not generating enough, would you have learned the right way to do it? You weren't successful straight off the bat. However, you did gain insights about what doesn't work, didn't you? Now you are armed with knowledge and wisdom about how to build a more engaged community of followers on Facebook! Don't let the fear of failure plunge you into inaction. You will learn nothing if you don't even attempt it.

Be proactive about your failures. In her bestselling book *How to Be a Bawsee* YouTube star and entertainer/performer, Lily Singh mentions about how she can never make the perfect omelets. By her own admission the eggs always break "into at least three pieces" Thereafter, instead of abandoning the less than perfect omelet, she treats herself to scrambled eggs by breaking them into even smaller pieces with a spatula.

Why should failure signify the dead end for an idea, venture or project? Gather your imperfect omelet and convert it into delicious scrambled eggs by being more proactive. At times, you may have to start all over again after witnessing failure. However, sometimes failure can also be the doorway to unexpected success. This likelier only when you have a more proactive approach to tackle challenges by their horns instead of sporting a reactive approach, where you blame everything around you for your failures.

Chapter Five: Success Habit Five - Laser Focus on a Single Task

Let us say you have 5 flower pots and a single can of water. You want to water all plants, but there's obviously not enough water for all. In a bid to water all the flowers pots, you divide the can of water equally them. Now, none of the flowering plants grow because there isn't enough water. Instead, if you would've used the can of water for a single flowering plant, it would've flourished. This is exactly how our time and efforts should be laser-focused on a single task to accomplish the best results.

Much like the can of water, we have limited time and energy. If we try to divide it between several tasks at a time, none of them will thrive. Impressive results need laser focus of energy, time and attention. There is only so much your brain can do when it comes to processing information, focusing on a task and implementing it to its fruition.

You can start as many businesses as you like. Starting businesses or new jobs doesn't have much life. The real value lays in finishing them or building them successfully. If you do too many things at a time, you are scattering your limited resources (think can of water) to nurture 10 different businesses, when the resources aren't sufficient to grow all businesses. Are all your businesses or ventures started together growing, offering value, accomplishing stellar results and more? Slim chance.

Apple CEO Time Cook once stated how Steve Jobs very clearly instilled within the organization the need to concentrate only on what each employee does best. Trust me, it is easy to keep adding to your job or business portfolio. It is challenging to stay focused to see one project to its successful completion. However, this is exactly what the wealthy and successful do. Though they have multiple businesses and sources of wealth, they seldom focus their effort and energies on more than a single task at a time.

Jobs once said in an interview to Fortune that "people think focus means saying yes to the thing you've got to focus on. But that's not what it means at all. It means saying no to the hundred other good ideas that there are. You have to pick carefully. This quote, in essence, sums up the importance of laser focusing – straight from the horse's mouth.

Henry Ford made wonderful cars. Picasso painted like a dream. Einstein excelled at these scientific theories. They did exceptionally well because they focused all their attention, energy and passion on a single thing at a time. Mark Zuckerberg focused all his energies on making Facebook one of the best social media platforms, while Bill Gates did the same for Microsoft. Same logic. If you fear being a one trick pony, take inspiration from the world's biggest brands. Think Starbucks espresso cafes, Coca-Cola and others.

I know, I know. You may be wracking your head hard to come up with names such as Warren Buffet and Richard Branson to challenge the 'laser focus' approach since they have diversified business interests. However, you should also know that Buffer spent about twenty years trying to get his feet wet in the investment market, while Branson concentrated exclusively on Virgin music for over a decade before moving conquering the airline industry.

Remember the magnifying glass example we discussed in a previous chapter. I want you to go back to it because it explains the power of laser focusing on a task brilliantly. When the light is spread or diffused, it serves no purpose. But when the same light is focused using a magnifying glass, it has the capacity to set a paper on fire. When the same light is even more focused through a laser beam, it can cut through steel. Similarly, you can accomplish the impossible when you laser-focus all your energy on completing a single task at a time.

See one project successfully through by investing all your energy, time and effort into it before you move to the next one. Avoid spreading yourself too thin with your limited attention, energy and time. You may end up launching 100 mediocre businesses (which is fine if you want a place in the Guinness Book of World Records), instead of one stellar, phenomenal venture you are proud of. Most wealthy and successful people focus on mastery. They give one business/project/job/venture their all before they are inspired to expand their legacy.

Here's why multitasking can be overhyped.

Our brains are not built to multitask

Human brains are programmed to focus on a single task at a time, and burdening it to perform several tasks at once only lowers its efficiency. The brain functions slowdown, which may impact the end result of each task. According to MIT neuroscientist Earl Miller, the human brain is "not wired to multitask well. When people think they are multitasking, they are actually switching from one task to another very rapidly. And every time they do, there is a cognitive cost."

So, in effect, when you think you are being extremely productive by doing several things at a time, you are paying the price of comprising on each of those tasks.

Constantly switching between tasks drops the momentum that builds when you do a single task for a longer period of time. When you switch between tasks, the momentum is disrupted, which means you have to start all over again when you come back. Focusing on a single task for a longer duration channelizes your cognitive powers exclusively on that task, thus avoiding cognitive disruption.

Think about it like this – you have a set of building blocks with which you are building a structure. You work on it diligently, given it all the time and attention it needs, one building block at a time. Then, suddenly something demands your attention. You shift focus to the new task, and the building blocks come crashing down like a pack of cards. You get back to building them once you are done with the new task.

However, now you don't have the same level of energy, enthusiasm and cognitive powers to build the blocks. The disruption in momentum that comes from continuously performing a task and building on it over a period of time hampers the end result! One of the worst brain habits is perpetually switching between tasks – something we proudly refer to as multitasking. When we try to finish a small task, let us say send an email or reply to a text message, our brains secrete dopamine (a feel-good reward hormone). Since the brain dollops of dopamine, we're led to constantly switch between small tasks that award us instant gratification.

For instance, when you are working writing a project, and you suddenly feel the urge to scan through your social media feed and comment on a few posts, your brain seeks instant gratification.

The most unfortunate part about this is that this process creates a feedback loop that gives us the impression that we are achieving a lot when in reality we are not accomplishing much or at least not fulfilling important tasks that need critical thinking.

It hampers your productivity and efficiency

It is tough to organize thoughts and filter irrelevant information when you multitask. The overall quality of your work suffers when you try to pack in too much within your brain's limited capacity.

Research conducted at the University of London revealed that people who multitasked while doing cognitive tasks witnesses a considerable drop in their Intelligence Quotient. The IQ level drops were similar to the ones people experience when they skip a night's sleep or intake marijuana. Scary, isn't it?

Multitasking also increases the brain's stress hormone – cortisol. When our brain constantly shifts gear between tasks, it pumps up higher levels of cortisol. This leaves us feeling mentally stressed and exhausted, even if your day has just started.

Who are the main culprits when it comes to demanding our time and attention? Emails and texts! Several studies have pointed to the conclusion that the constant thrill of checking bolded, unread emails from the inbox or texts (which typically demand immediacy) keeps us forever distracted from focusing on productive tasks.

To avoid, create an email schedule. Instead of having the momentum robbed off your task each time to reply to an email or task, designate a time to send/reply to all emails together. This way, you are not shifting between tasks every 10 minutes. Send or reply to all your emails at the beginning or end of the day (or anytime in between). However, reserve a fixed time for it. Similarly, unless it's urgent (in which case people can call you anyway), resist the urge to reply to text messages until lunch or at the end of the day. This is just one of the several strategies used by the wealthy and successful to stay productive.

If you want to focus on the task at hand, turn off notifications from your emails, social media apps, and texts. Research conducted by McKinsey Global Institute Study revealed that workers spend 28 percent of their working hours during a week checking emails. The multitasking massacre is real. Designate specific timings for each type of task by clubbing similar tasks together.

It slows you down

Contrary to popular perception, multitasking doesn't save time. It'll take you more to complete two projects if you switch between them than if you tackle each one separately. This is also true of drivers who take much longer to reach their destination when they chat on mobile phones.

If you really want to save time, avoid multitasking. Instead, perform tasks by clubbing them together in batches. For instance, pay all bills online together at one time or clear all invoices together once a week/forthright/month.

The thing is, every task requires a given mindset. Once you get into the flow of this specific mindset and suddenly take on another task, the brain shifts gear and experiences a change in the mindset to readjust to the new task. This takes you longer to complete both the tasks because you've to keep spending time to get into the groove of both mindsets constantly. Instead, stay on one task at a time and complete it before moving to the next.

You'll end up making more mistakes

Really now if you fancy yourself as a superwoman or man who is capable of juggling multiple tasks at a time, rework your strategy. Shuffling between tasks can cause your productivity to plunge by a whopping 40 percent. It can also increase chances of errors, more so if these tasks involve an increased amount critical thinking.

In a study conducted in France (2010), it was discovered that the human brain is capable of handling only a couple of complex tasks without much trouble. This is because our brain has two distinct lobes that can divide tasks equally between them. When you add an additional task, it puts pressure on your frontal cortex, which can result in a higher number errors.

If you want to be more productive and minimize errors, focus all your energy, time and efforts on a single task at a time.

You lose out of life

Imagine trying to do everything at one and not having the time to enjoy the result of your efforts. Forget about stopping to smell the roses or watching butterflies and the rainbow. Multitaskers don't even see things that are right before them. A study conducted by the Western Washington University I'm 2009 revealed that 75 percent of college students who strolled across the campus square didn't even notice a vibrantly dressed clown while speaking on their cell phones. In effect, the students were looking at their surroundings. However, none of its registered owing to the inattentional blindness - as the researchers termed it. You miss out being more mindful of the present or experiences in and around you when you are preoccupied with too many things.

Can you focus on your food and eat more mindfully when you are busy sending emails while grabbing a sandwich on your desk? Can you enjoy a walk in the woods if you are busy scrolling through your social media feed while walking? Multitasking takes away the mindfulness and purposefulness from what you are doing. Thus, you are losing out on living in the present or savoring the given moment.

The entire world is waking up to the goodness of mindfulness, which is nothing but being purposeful and intentional about soaking in the present moment in a non-judgmental manner. By doing too many things at a time, you are not focusing mindfully on a single task. You may be physically present, but you aren't really soaking in the moment or mentally present enough to experience the moment to its fullest. Being mindful means even when you are overcome by the urge to focus on multiple tasks, you simply acknowledge these distracting thoughts and redirect focus back to the present task or the highest priority task at hand. Instead of pushing these disturbing and distracting feelings from the mind, you simply acknowledge them, allow them to live their time, and then gently focus attention back to what you are doing. Practice mindful meditation to increase your span of attention, concentration, and focus.

Mindful meditation involves sitting in a comfortable posture in a distraction-free place to focus on your breathing. Put all electronic devices on silent and eliminate all distractions. Sit in a calm and serene space. Relax your body and mind. Start focusing on your breath. Notice the inhalation and exhalation patterns. Count and draw long breaths by keenly focusing on every inhalation and exhalation.

Notice the feeling of air making its way into your mouth, throat, lungs, and stomach. How does your body feel with each inhalation and exhalation? There will be a bunch of distracting thoughts that will attempt to take away focus from your breathing. However, acknowledge these thoughts briefly and let them pass before redirecting focus on the breath.

Multitasking hampers creativity and the vital 'aha' moments

Multitasking needs plenty of working memory or short-term brain storage. When the entire working memory is utilized, it hampers starts affecting your creativity. This was established at a research conducted by the University of Illinois in Chicago. Too much pressure and focus on the working memory can actually end up harming our performance where creative problem solving is concerned.

Multitaskers are often robbed off intuitions, daydreams, and those snap 'aha' moments. There is little spontaneity and "eureka" moments of revelation because the creativity is clouded by performing too many tasks at a time. You are more tuned in to your creativity and inner self when your brain is not overwhelmed by several tasks.

Thoughts, ideas, and solutions follow freely when you are more connected to your creative, inner self. If you want to bring greater spontaneity in your thought process and ideas, start doing less or focus on one thing at a time. Daydreams, intuition and Aha moments are closely linked with our subconscious mind. When you focus on doing too many things at once, you are breaking the connection between your conscious and subconscious mind, thus robbing you of precious spontaneity and more intuitively driven actions/decisions.

The focus is on information and intention rather than results

Our entire life is spent filling our brains with information and intention without focusing on results from the information or intention overload. Despite making effort, we experience less than flattering results. Of course, at times the situation is beyond our control. We can't do much about changing market dynamics that impact our business or varying trends impacting buyer preferences as an entrepreneur.

However, what we can do is strengthen our efforts by avoiding scattered or fragmented attention. We are in control of ensuring that our energy isn't diffused on multiple tasks that award us less than flattering results. Remember the flower pot analogy? Un-compound your attention, focus, energy, and efforts! Clump them together on a single activity if you want to increase your chances of success.

How do you light a fire? You bundle up all the available tinder and light it. You don't go around lighting fire across a hundred grass blades throughout the field. Concentrate on that one spark it takes to burn the bunch of tinder instead of trying to light fifty different things at once. Don't get me wrong – rich and successful people don't put all their eggs in one basket. However, they seldom fill all their baskets together.

By all means, build multiple sources of income, varied enterprises or investment channels. However, it is crucial to laser focus your efforts, time and energy purposefully on one task at a time. Let's say you are in the gym for the first time. There's a barbell, kettlebell or any other fitness equipment you fancy before you. There are plenty of thoughts circulating in your mind. What exactly is the weight on that bar? How do I place my feet? Where should my hands be? Then there's a ton of other unrelated stuff going on in your head. Did I lock bolt the house door while coming? Is my car locked? When is the project I am currently working on due? Did I deposit the last check I received from the client? Have I worn by t-shirt backward? The underpants hurt as hell!

Too many thoughts resulting in scattered attention. Now take all this attention, focus and energy and invest it in a single task, idea or thought. Finish it before moving on to the next.

Scattered attention will give you scattered results, which isn't the best success policy. You need to give every task you take on the best chance of success!

Tips to increase your focus and eliminate distractions

1. Create a schedule for distractions

We all have those niggling little distractions that award us instant gratification or pleasure. Having fun conversations with co-workers, checking our social media feed, listening to music, checking out the latest collection on your favorite e-commerce site. It's achingly enjoyable, I know. However, one of the biggest reasons why some people are roaringly successful while others barely manage to scrape through life is because the former club has mastered the art of delaying gratification.

Giving in to instant pleasures can cause your focus and performance to nose-dive. Plus, you may not enjoy your pleasurable distractions as much if you do them smack in the middle of an important project (at the back of your mind you know there's something important to be finished). So why not factoring in a separate schedule for these distractions rather than comprise both on your work and leisure? Don't deny yourselves the little joys of life. Instead, schedule a separate time for them.

Once you finish working on the current task at hand or writing a few pages, go and grab a cup of coffee or catch up with co-workers. When you set clear task completion goals, you will be even more motivated to finish it. It's like bribing yourself to complete a task quickly so you can then go and enjoy your pleasurable little distractions.

2. You aren't cooking stew

There are tons of things that happen to us each day which set a positive or negative momentum for the day. It is human nature to obsess over the negative and keep stewing it in minds. When things don't go as we want them to, we keep focusing on it for extended periods. At times, the small and inconsequential things occupy more attention than they deserve.

You are cooking stew on slow flame! Things can go wrong but to fuss over them for longer than you need simply expends your time, energy and focus, thus spilling over its unfortunate effects into another task. Stop right there! Don't let one negative thing someone said or did impact all that you've planned to go ahead.

Your phone may have stopped working, or your boss may have chided you for not doing the latest project as well as you did the earlier ones. For the former, instead of fussing over the phone for long, you take a few minutes to figure out if you can rectify it. If not, you contact the company to look into the issue. When your boss says, you didn't do as well in the latest project as they had expected, you focus on the current task at hand

and maybe rework on the earlier project once this one's done.

Focus on what needs to be done not what is beyond you (phone repair) or something that's already been done (project). Take action in the right direction or have a plan in place to rectify it when something bothers you instead of overthinking or obsessing about it.

3. Don't open what you don't need

Sometimes I see a million tabs open on the computers of people complaining about how they are having a hard time focusing on their work. Buddy, if you don't need those tabs or applications, why open them? Don't log in to your email on the computer if you don't need it while working on something more important. If you don't need to know about the next big flash sale, don't open your favorite shopping site.

Golden rule – don't open anything you don't need while working on your system. When social media platforms, applications, and multiple tabs are not open on your system, it is easier to concentrate on the task you are trying to complete on your computer.

The risk of being distracted is even greater when you are working from home or a café. If you are at the café, don't get the Wi-Fi access code if you don't need the internet. You'll be likelier to focus on your work in the face of reduced distractions.

There are several handy applications that can temporarily block your social media accounts to prevent you from being distracted. For instance, SelfControl allows you to select websites you want to browse for a set time.

4. Make yourself unavailable

Yes, your office hours are scheduled to prevent distractions. However, you should also schedule time when you are unavailable to eliminate distractions. One of my friends who is a manager at a top firm hired a coach to help improve his time management. The first thing the coach asked him to do was take a couple of hours each day to completely cut from everything and everyone.

The door to his cabin would be closed, the telephone would be off the hook, and he had to make it clear to his staff that he wasn't available during those two hours unless it was an emergency. Using this technique, my friend was able to accomplish more in those two hours than he would in the entire days earlier. This is the power of laser focus and avoiding scattered attention or distractions.

Working long hours is terribly hyped. It isn't something one should be proud of. It simply means you weren't able to manage your efficiency and productivity, which is why the hours got stretched. You really don't need to be efficient for the entire 8 hours to be a good worker. If you perform at your optimal level of efficiency even for a couple of hours each day, without any distractions, you accomplish a major chunk of your day's task. Focus on the most crucial tasks to be completed while going distraction-free or making yourself unavailable and you'll be blown by how much you can get done!

5. See the task through

Do you ever feel like you are making superb progress with a task and then suddenly experience the urge to take a break? You can go on that break, which spans longer than you planned and get back to the task. When you pick up from where you left, you realize you've lost momentum. It will now take you some time to get into the groove of the task to reach the point you were at when you left for a break. We do this, often unaware, several times throughout the day. A quick call, checking social media on an impulse, heading out for a coffee break – at times we don't even consider it a break.

Break down every task by focusing on it and seeing it through to its completion before you move on to the next milestone or take a break. See the task through to its completion before you take your break. This allows you to recharge your batteries after completing one task and approach the new one with a fresh and rejuvenated mind.

6. Check the temperature

No, this isn't about how angry or cool you are. It is about the temperature of your immediate work environment. A Cornell University study found that the efficiency of workers is at its peak and they tend to make fewer mistakes when the temperature is between 68 and 77 degrees. When it's too cold or too hot, our focus/productivity can be hampered. Another piece if research conducted by the Helsinki Institute of Technology revealed that the magic figure is 71 degrees. You may not be able to control the workplace thermostat. Bring some warm attire or fans!

7. Keep a clutter-free desk

It is easy to feel distracted or experience the urge to multitask when your desk is filled with plenty of unwanted stuff. Plus, you'll spend plenty of time looking for something you really need because there's ton of stuff you don't need. Take the time to organize your desk for success. File all your papers in different folders by categorizing them. Make a place for all the knick-knacks. Don't keep anything you don't need right away on the desk or work table. This will keep you stay focused on the tasks that need to be completed immediately without distractions.

8. Train People or set ground rules

A major part of our distraction comes from other people. There are constant interruptions, disturbances, and distractions in the form of other people in our daily lives. The smartest way to prevent this and focus on energies on the task at hand is to set ground rules and communicate them clearly to everyone. Politely and assertively explain to them that you would appreciate if they don't interrupt you and respect your need to focus on the task by reducing communication with you during designated time blocks.

9. Identify tasks that need your focus

I've found a lot of success when it comes to prioritizing what needs my immediate focus or attention using the four-quadrant method. Yes, it has been sufficiently established by now that doing too many tasks at a time isn't a very good idea and laser focus can help you win the day.

Make our columns in a notebook/notes application each day. They should be urgent and important, important but not urgent, urgent but not important, and not important not urgent. Classify all your impending tasks into each of these four quadrants. All your energies should be focused on tasks that are urgent and important, followed by important but not urgent, urgent but not important and finally, not important not urgent.

Let us say you have to make a presentation before a prospective client who can give you a lot of business in a couple of days. This is urgent and important. If a company whose product/service you are using asks you to send in a feedback/review of their product or service, it may be urgent because it comes with a timeline. But is it important to you? Nope! You can very well skip it for something that is more important even if it isn't high priority. The least efforts, energy, and resources should be expended on tasks that are neither urgent nor important. When you identify tasks based on their priority, it is easier to laser focus on the right tasks.

At the beginning of each day of work, I have a ready list of the day's most important and urgent tasks to begin. Break away from the multitasking myth. It doesn't speed productivity. If anything, it slows your outcome, which will be much more powerful if your light is laser-focused on a single task.

Chapter Six: Success Habit Six - Time is Money

"Every day is a bank account, and time is our currency. No one is rich, no one is poor, we've got 24 hours each." —Christopher Rice

If you want to know a person's true personality, mindset, chances of success or character, ask them how they utilize their free time. You'll be blown by the insights. Successful people will always utilize their time optimally to stay productive and ahead of their game! They will spend time reading, learning, acquiring varied skills that help them become more efficient and so on. On the other hand, your average Joes will binge watch Netflix series (not that I am not a fan), surf the web pointlessly and stay married to their PlayStation. You'll seldom find the hustlers spending hours on social media checking people's newsfeed.

Time is true wealth as time once gone can never come back. Every person (successful, failure, rich, poor) has 24 hours in a day. Hustlers or successful people don't have any more time than you do. However, what distinguishes them from the rest is how they utilize this limited time to create optimal results and stay productive. Here are some of my most awesome time management secrets that you can start implementing right away.

1. Be a 5 am person or early starter. I could author an entire book about the benefits of being a 5 am person. Some of the world's most successful and wealthy people begin their day early to pack much more into it. Be an early riser if you want to get more done during the day. Of course, early to bed and early to rise has several physical and mental health benefits.

When you begin early, you get a major part of your work done by midday, which keeps you comfortably on course with the day's engagements. Besides, when you get a lot done during the early part of the day, you are bound to stay motivated, positive and energetic throughout the day. You'll feel encouraged to keep going because you've accomplished quite a lot, and this will result in higher productivity.

Another time management technique practiced by many successful people is aiming to complete the toughest and most time-consuming tasks of their day during the first half of the day. Once you finish the day's most challenging tasks, it sets a positive momentum for tasks to follow, which in comparison are much simpler than the ones you just handled. This will leave you feeling even more inspired and energized about finishing the remaining tasks. When you know you have a fairly long day ahead or plenty of tasks to tackle, sleep early. Waking up with a fresh mind after a good 8-10 hours of sleep keeps you mentally active, positive and enthusiastic.

2. Utilize your effective hours optimally. Try to schedule your most challenging tasks during your peak hours. Each person will have their own peak hours, which is the time of the day when you are most active and effective. For instance, if

you are an early morning person, use the time when everyone is asleep to finish your most challenging tasks. Don't use it to reply to emails. Identify a time when you are most productive during the day, and do more during this time frame. Leave the not so important tasks for your leaner moments during the day. Say, if you are never in your element post lunch, utilize that time for relatively relaxed tasks such as sending emails.

3. Leverage time, efforts and skills by delegating tasks. If you are one of those stubborn old-school entrepreneurs who want to single-handedly take the credit for building and running a successful business, sorry to burst your bubble. There is only so much you can accomplish by doing things singlehandedly. Even if you work round the clock, you have only 24 hours a day, and there's only so much you can accomplish by working alone for those 24 hours. This means if you are trading time for money, you are going to make money for a maximum of 24 hours/day.

However, smart wealth creators recognize the power of leveraging other people's time, efforts and skills for their wealth creation. They realize that if they have to build wealth over a period of time, they need to hire services of other people or delegate tasks instead of being a one-man army. If you run the marathon, you will burn yourself out faster than you realize. However, if you run a relay, you'll increase your chances of winning.

Scaling up a business or project requires utilization of other people's time, efforts and skills. Think about the difference between putting in 24 hours of work and getting paid for those 24 hours, and hiring 5 people who work for 8 hours each and getting paid for 40 hours of work. Even after factoring expenses related to the workforce, you may most likely end up making much more than if you work alone. This is the way smart visionaries operate. Leveraging other people's time and efforts is important to the process of wealth creation.

4. Use the popular Pomodoro time management method. The Pomodoro time management method is widely used across the world for increasing productivity and eliminating wasteful utilization of time. It is in effect also relevant to the previous chapter where we discussed about hyper-focusing on a single task to accomplish better results. This time management technique was conceived by Francesco Cirillo in the early 80's. Pomodoro literally translates into tomato in Italian, and since Cirillo utilized a timer shaped like a tomato, the technique became popular as the Pomodoro technique.

How does it work?

To begin with, you set a 25-minute timer and work on a task uninterrupted for the next 25 minutes. Once you complete a single Pomodoro cycle (each cycle is of 25 minutes), you award yourself a brief 4-5-minute break or breather. This is followed by the next Pomodoro cycle and a subsequent 4-5-minute break. Once you finish 4 Pomodoro cycles with a break of 45 minutes between them, you give yourself a 15-20-minute break.

If you finish a task before a 25-minute Pomodoro cycle is up, the remaining time has to be devoted towards reading and learning. Other tasks that demand your attention need to wait until you complete the present Pomodoro cycle.

The primary objective of this highly effective time management technique is optimizing productivity by eliminating distractions and focusing on a single task at a time. When you work on a task uninterrupted for 25 minutes, you keep the momentum, focus, and efficiency going. Nothing hampers the continuity of your current task, which increases your overall productivity. Short breaks leave you feeling rejuvenated and refreshed to take on the next task or batch of work with greater clarity, concentration and focus. Also, using a time induces a sense of urgency, where feel the need to finish a task without distractions. This means you avoid over fussing about perfection or spending more time on a task than required, similar to a timed examination. The Pomodoro method, among other things, help a person develop more willpower, concentration, discipline, and self-control.

5. Have everything in order the previous day. I'd need a million hands if I counted on my fingers the number of times I've had a bad or inefficient day simply because I didn't prepare for it the day before in the days I'd just started my professional life. It has happened with the best of us. You wake up late on the day of your interview or presentation and end up grumpy and cranky. You feel out of control, and things quickly spiral downward. There is a presentation scheduled at the beginning of day, but you locate the pen drive now. You were working on it until last evening and now cannot find it.

To save yourself all the stress, hassle and anxiety, and conserve your energy for more productive tasks, have everything ready the day before. Let's say you have to begin writing a report the next day. Keep your research, and all relevant documents ready the night before. This way you won't spend time looking for documents. It'll be a huge time saver if you can get to work straight away. Have your clothes, documents, planners, pen drives, digital files and more ready to being working. Other than saving time, the approach allows you to perform your task in a more stress-free manner.

6. Use your waiting time wisely. You'll be blown away by how much you manage you accomplish simply by utilizing your waiting time more productively. Next time you are waiting for a movie to begin at the multiplex or for your bus or at the doctor's – try researching/writing a rough draft for your next project, reading something inspiring, generating ideas and so on. Don't have time to read? How about listening to eBooks or podcasts while traveling to and from work?

We can get a lot done by using the buffer time between activities. Whenever I had some free time before an upcoming presentation, I'd spend time adding brief points about what I wanted to cover in it. I also like watching motivational videos and sending emails during my filler waiting time. These time gaps are enough to complete your tail end tasks, leaving a major chunk of your actual work time free for more productive tasks.

Have you heard of Okenski's two-minute rule? I swear by it. It states that it can complete any task in less than two minutes, it should be done instantly. Olenski, who devised the two-minute rule, believes if we finish something immediately, it takes much less time to do something as opposed to putting it off for another time.

7. Use the 80-20 Pareto principle for identifying and increasing most productive tasks. The 80-20 Pareto principle states that 20 percent of our entire efforts contribute to about 80 percent of our results. Nail down these 20 percent tasks and spend more time doing these to increase your productivity.

Identify and discard time wasters that do not contribute meaningfully towards your goals. Resist the urge to scan through your social media feed every few minutes, watch television, play games, and replace it with more productive activities that contribute to overall results.

Let us assume that you spend 20 percent of your time making sales presentations for prospective clients. This contributes towards 80 percent of your entire sales revenue. However, you spend a major portion of time sending and receiving emails from online clients, who contribute to a small percentage of your sales revenue.

Wouldn't it be more sensible to increase the time spent on major revenue generating activities (in this case presentations) rather than activities that contribute a small percentage to the overall sales (emails)? You can delegate the task of sending and receiving emails to someone else while increasing the amount of hours spent giving presentations. This is how the rich and successful make the most of their time.

8. Kill procrastination. Do not save reading this for later. Read it right away. Read and begin practicing this almost immediately. There are plenty of ways to overcome procrastination. My favorite tip is to break big tasks into smaller deadlines. If you have to deliver a 49-page report in the next 7 days, don't wait until the sixth day to write a hurried report. Also, don't keep telling yourself that it's a 7-day deadline. Instead, keep a daily deadline of writing 7 pages, and meet it on an everyday basis. You'll stop running around like your tail is on fire at the last minute if you create daily deadlines and shorter milestones for big projects or goals.

Avoid over-analyzing and delaying something due to an obsession with perfection. You'll never get it right until you begin. We keep telling ourselves we'll start something when we know all we can about it. Another stupid excuse! Start and learn when you act upon it.

Optimize your space for facilitating greater productivity, and avoiding inaction, lethargy, inertia, lack of motivation and so on. Keep your social media apps on silent, don't allow people to walk into your cabin.

Penalize yourself every time you fail to finish a task on time or give in to the urge to procrastinate. Put $10 away in a box for each instance of failing to complete a job or procrastination. At the end of every month or two months, hand it over to a cause you absolutely despise.

Similarly, reward yourself when you manage to finish a task on time. It can be treating yourself to cup of your favorite coffee or a Netflix show you enjoy watching or buying yourself a book you always wanted to read. The idea of enjoying an interesting activity once you complete the task at hand gives you something to look forward to. This makes them monstrous, mundane task more doable. Completing a task will seem less of drudgery if you offer yourself some incentive to complete it.

9. Learn to say a firm and polite no. Don't try to be a people pleaser by saying yes to everyone and burning yourself out or take away time from your goals. I am not advocating being an unhelpful and mean individual. Extending a helping hand is great but not at the cost of your own efficiency, goals, and productivity. Differentiate between instances where people genuinely need your help and where they take advantage of you. I've come across tons of lazy sloths who don't want to do their work themselves and often take your courtesy for granted.

Be in control of activities you wish to invest your time on. If you aren't up for a task, don't say yes to it. People may utilize a bunch of subtle persuasion and manipulation strategies. Stay true to your resolve. Don't lock your time for meeting other people's goals. Say a polite and assertive no without sounding apologetic or regretful about it.

Stay aware of the consequences of meeting other people's requests. At times, people will follow smaller requests with bigger ones. Respect your time to allow others to respect it, and spend more time on hustling.

Chapter Seven: Success Habit Seven – Perseverance

"I fear not the man who has practiced 10,000 kicks once, but I fear the man who has practiced one kick 10,000 times." – Bruce Lee

If you ask me about that one quality that separates successful people from failures, it is perseverance. This one trait alone has the ability seal your fortune or take you to great heights of success. Successful people do not quit. Period. They take their challenges head on and keep going until they witness the success they are destined for. Instead of ruminating about their failures they hold it by their horns and transform it into success.

Thomas Edison is one of the best examples of determination and perseverance. He was an inventor credited for multiple patents and ingenious innovations. Edison is well-known as the inventor of the light bulb. However, it didn't happen overnight. It took years of research, experimenting, and theories to get it right.

The prolific inventor whom everyone admires conducted more than 9,000 failed experiments before he perfected it. On being asked why Edison was putting intense effort into the process of creating a light bulb without witnessing any results, he replied, "I have got results! I know several thousand ways that won't work!" This is what perseverance is about.

Have you hit the gym or worked on toning/building your body? Are muscles built overnight? Nope, it takes several days, disciplined habits, the appropriate coping mechanisms and will to overcome obstacles. Similarly, building the perseverance muscle requires a more conscious transformation in your actions, thoughts, mindset, beliefs, and attitude.

Here are some powerful ways to build your perseverance and determination muscle.

1. Push yourself little by little each day. Making small increments in your progress daily is a great way to build perseverance. Let say you walk 2 miles each day or do 100 push-ups a day. Try increasing this number gradually. Walk for an extra half a mile or try accommodating 110 push-ups in your workout. Small laps will increase your capacity to run for longer without feeling exhausted. The objective is to push yourself into doing more by getting out of your comfort zone. If you are comfortable writing 15 pages a day, push yourself into doing 17-18. Gradually, increase this to 20 pages a day. Keep building on your capacity to sustain. Push yourself slowly to avoid a burnout.

2. Deal with any crisis in a logical, balanced and cool way. There isn't a need to create a soap opera or saga out of everything in your life. Deal with challenges in a logical and rational manner. Stress is an inevitable component of any successful person's life. Where is there is success, wealth and glory, there is bound to be added responsibility, exhaustion, and stress.

Sometimes, circumstances are outside our control. However, the manner in which we choose to respond to our circumstances determine the influence they have over us.

3. Develop a solid support system. Build a positive, powerful and inspiring support system to derive strength from when needed. During challenging times, you should be able to share your feelings with a close-knit, trustworthy and encouraging group of people. Exchange your thoughts, enlist their support, learn about their journey, gain positive feedback, receive support and talk about possible solutions. You'll end up gaining an altogether different perspective about a situation.

Talking to trusted people can offer you new insights, perspectives, and solutions about challenges, which in turn increases your perseverance power. Merely hanging out with people who are positive, inspiring and supportive helps you overcome disturbing, negative situations. When you are filled with self-doubt, these supportive people will dispel your incorrect notions by encouraging you. They'll offer you a more balanced and less catastrophic reality check.

4. Take a break. If your challenges seem too overwhelming to continue, rest for a while or take a short break instead of quitting. Imagine if you were just inches away from success or your destination after walking for several thousand miles, and you just give up because you are tired of walking any further. How unfortunate would that be? Success is often closer than we believe. If only you would've taken the last few steps, you would've been a huge success. When something doesn't accomplish the intended results, try taking a break and changing your strategy instead of simply giving up. Approach the task with a fresh and brand-new perspective after a break. True success comes to people who avoid giving up.

One of the world's all-time best selling and richest author J.K. Rowling (Harry Potter fame) had her Harry Potter manuscript rejected by a whopping 12 publishers before Bloomsbury decided to go ahead with publishing a few copies. Would she have attained the wealth, glory and success she does today if she'd let those 12 rejections determine her destiny? Would several million readers across the planet enjoy her writing if she's let a handful of people evaluate her ability?

Irrespective of past failures, success may be much closer than you believe. Take time off if you feel tired or stressed. However, don't quit. You wouldn't have anything from Windows to Disneyland to the light bulb to planes to Facebook to iPhones if their founders that quit owing to early failures and disappointments. Instead of seeing failures as obstacles to your success, see view them as stepping stones that take you closer to success.

Imagine a scenario where you are required to cover a considerable distance on foot. You continue walking a long distance but feel tired after a while. What do you do? You go back the entire journey or do you just halt for a while and continue? The journey of your life isn't any different. Success can be nearer than you think!

5. Develop a solution mindset. The reason some people are overcome by their problems is because they view it simply as that – a problem or roadblock. View challenges and obstacles from a solutions perspective. The lack of ability to come up with solutions is what drives people to throw in the towel. When faced with a challenge, brainstorm. Come up with a bunch of solutions, ideas, and possibilities for resolving it. Maybe you need a change in the approach or a slight tweak in strategy. Identify different ways to overcome a challenging or overwhelming situation.

In fact, go a step ahead and think of solutions for problems or challenges that can possibly arise. Have solutions, and a plan B ready! Your confidence will increase when you have more practical and workable solutions at your disposal. Develop the ability to think out of the box solutions.

6. Develop a sense of humor. This is so easy and enjoyable, yet people fail to cash in on it. When tough times fall upon you, humor can sail you through. Looking at the lighter side of situation helps overcome stress and anxiety related to it. You gather a different and refreshing perspective about challenges.

Similarly, when we catch a funny film, read a laugh-a-minute book or attend a stand-up comedy gig or spend time with humorous people, our dopamine (feel-good hormone) levels rise. This, in turn, boosts your brain's fighting mechanism. Balance tough situations with enjoyable things that save you from despair and depression. Don't let negative situations consume you or take them increasingly seriously.

Look at the brighter, lighter side of things and laugh. Developing a sense of humor may not make your problem any smaller. However, it'll increase your ability to cope with the challenge. Wealth and successful people understand that the path to success is filled with challenges, and they have their coping mechanisms ready.

7. Develop a positive perspective about your skills and abilities. A person's self-esteem and self-image impact, to a huge extent, their ability to stay perseverant. Remind yourself of your strengths, accomplishments, skills and glorious moments. Make a list of challenging situations you faced earlier, and how you overcame them. Draw inspiration from positive moments.

Sign up for public speaking courses to boost your confidence. Attend networking events, seminars and workshops to meet positive people who make you feel good about yourself. Similarly, master new skills that will increase your confidence, self-esteem, and will-power! Sometimes, all you need is a little creativity venting. Try redecorating a space, writing a short story or penning a poem.

8. Watch your self-talk. What's your mental chatter like? If it isn't aligned for positivity,

wealth and success, you'd better retune it to another frequency. Our self-talk can make or break our success chances. It can help you sail through tough situations or plunge you into failure. Modify your self-talk for success by making it more constructive and positive. You've heard the famous quote by now, "thoughts become things." If your mental chatter is more self-defeatist, success will definitely evade you!

In place of saying, "I can never do this," say, "This may not be easy, but that doesn't stop me from giving it my best. It is only a matter of time I master it."

Stop yourself in the tracks with a physical action (snap a rubber band on your hand, pinch yourself, whack yourself on the head, bite your tongue – do whatever you want) each time you engage in negative or can't-do mental talk.

Replace negative words and phrases with more positive terms. Let your inner voice guide you towards positivity and possibilities. Avoid speaking in fixed or absolute terms such as something can never be done. Keep options open, and explore alternatives. Tell yourself, "every step takes me closer to my dream" or "I am truly happy and grateful to be able to learn this lesson."

Another thing to guard against is catastrophizing events or imagining the worst. A few challenges and failures in the past do not mean you will fail at everything you do. This isn't a realistic thinking. Don't allow a few challenges to deter your spirit! Avoid personalizing your failures or blaming yourself for them. Rise above them by finding evidence to the contrary. Think about all the times you've been successful. Each time you think something cannot be done, go back to an instance where you believed you couldn't do something and ended up mastering it.

What is the primary source of your negative self-talk? Is it originating from people surrounding you? Are you spending more time with people who urge you to give up on your dreams? Are they gnawing on your sense of self-worth and self-esteem by doubting your abilities? When people say something cannot be done, they are talking about their inability to do it. It doesn't define necessarily define your abilities. Stay away from folks who derail you from your goals because it invariably impacts your self-talk.

Bonus Chapter: Patience is a Virtue

Have you ever seen a Chinese bamboo tree? Like every tree in the world, it needs water, soil and sunshine to grow. However, during the first year of planting it, you'll see no signs of activity. The plant is barely visible below the soil. Again, in the second year, no above the soil growth! However, the nurturing continues. It is given fertile soil, lots of water and sunshine. During the third and fourth year, no visible growth signs again. You'll begin to wonder if the nurturing (water, soil, sunshine) is having any effect on it at all.

Then a miracle happens in the fifth year. Lo and behold, the Chinese bamboo tree suddenly grows a whopping 80 feet tall in the next six to eight weeks. Yes, almost no growth for 4 years, and then suddenly 80 feet in 2 months alone!

Now, kid me not by telling me that the bamboo tree grew 80 feet only as a result of those six to eight weeks. Do you really believe it was lying inactive for the first four years, and then suddenly grew during the fifth year? Or was it developing and growing a powerful root system underground for four years to prepare for an exponential growth during the fifth year and thereafter?

We all know the answer. If the bamboo tree hadn't developed a strong, invisible foundation during its growth years, it would've never been able to sustain its exponential growth. The outward growth is only after the fourth year, but that doesn't mean it wasn't growing internally for the first four years.

The same holds true for your success. You may keep hustling and building without visible results for long. However, this patient toiling towards your dreams and goals is building your business/work and your character. You are growing a strong character by overcoming challenges. You are slowly yet steadily building a get rich sure business or career instead of a get rich quick scheme, which seldom sustains in the long run. Building a strong internal foundation needs endless patience.

Had you dug up the bamboo seed each year to check if it was growing, you would've stunted its growth.

A caterpillar is resigned to its doomed destiny on the ground if it seeks to free itself from a struggle inside the cocoon. However, if it sustains its struggle inside the cocoon, it transforms into a beautiful creature that can fly.

You may not see visible instances of progress while continuously spending time, effort and other resources on building your dream. However, if you show patience and keep working on your goal, much like the bamboo tree, you may witness a sudden and exponential growth in future. Building your dream with patience is the key to being wealthy and successful!

Conclusion

Thank you for downloading this book.

I hope it was able to help you learn more about success habits, self-discipline, getting into wealth creation mindset and practical strategies through which you can accomplish the success, wealth and life mastery you are destined to achieve. I have included innumerable action plans, practical strategies and proven techniques for developing greater productivity, efficiency and a success mindset, which will help you achieve your financial and success goals. Identify your definition of success, fulfillment, and happiness, and work consciously towards it by following the strategies mentioned in this book.

The book is packed with plenty of time management, goal fulfillment, productivity-boosting, creation mindset and other valuable success and mindset hacks that will help you get on the wealth, success and life mastery lane straightaway.

The next step is to take action. A person who does not read is as good as a person who cannot read. Similarly, knowledge without action is pointless. One cannot achieve success, mastery, and prosperity simply by reading about it and feeling great. You have to go out there and put it into practice to make it work! You have to sweat it out and give it your all to emerge a winner!

Lastly, if you enjoyed reading the book, please take some time to share your views and post a review. It'd be highly appreciated.

Here's to your success, wealth and life mastery!